Table of Contents

Taming the Intraday Trading Beast: Introducing the Tripod Strategy

Picture this: You're staring at a stock chart, prices are jumping like a popcorn machine - one minute it's skyrocketing, the next it's crashing. That's the world of intraday trading, exciting, nerve-wracking, and a recipe for disastrous decisions if you don't have a plan.

We've all been there - making hasty trades based on gut feelings, getting whipsawed by the market...it's enough to make anyone want to chuck their computer out the window.

Stability Matters: The Power of Three

That's why I developed the Tripod Strategy. Think of a tripod - it's solid, it won't tip over. Same concept here, but instead of legs, we've got three powerful tools:

- **Central Pivot Range (CPR):** We use yesterday's price action to predict today's potential trading zones.

- **20-Period Exponential Moving Average (EMA):** Shows us which way the tide's moving and helps us ride the trend.
- **Support and Resistance:** These levels reveal where the tug-of-war between buyers and sellers gets serious, giving us entry and exit clues.

It's Not Just About Charts

Look, a strategy is only as good as the trader using it. That's why this book isn't just about pretty chart setups. We're diving into:

- **Mental Fortitude:** How to control emotions and stick to the plan, no matter what.
- **Risk Management:** Protecting your hard-earned cash is priority number one.
- **Adapting to the Market:** Not every day is tradeable - we'll learn when to step back and observe.
- **The Power of Backtesting:** Let's see how the strategy stacks up before risking real money.

This Isn't a Magic Bullet...

...but it's a heck of a good guide. Intraday trading isn't easy; it takes discipline, practice, and a willingness to accept that losses are part of the game. The Tripod Strategy can't eliminate risk, but it can give you a serious edge.

So, if you're tired of watching profits vanish before your eyes, or feel like the market is playing you instead of the other way around, keep reading. Let's turn you into a disciplined, savvy intraday trader.

Throughout this book, you'll find numerous charts to illustrate the concepts and principles of the Tripod Strategy. While color charts can certainly enhance visual understanding, I've opted to use black and white charts for this resource. This decision aims to keep the cost of the book accessible to a wider audience. If you prefer color charts or would like access to my daily chart updates, please feel free to contact me at

thetripodtrader@gmail.com.

CPR – Your Secret Weapon for Intraday Trading

If you hate staring at charts without a clue where the action's gonna happen, CPR is your new best friend. Think of it like this: every stock has invisible zones where the fight between buyers and sellers is likely to go down. These zones are drawn from yesterday's trading session, and CPR (Central Pivot Range) helps you find them.

CPR isn't Magic, It's Just Math (thankfully)

No voodoo here. CPR uses three pieces of data:

- **Yesterday's High**: The mountaintop the price reached.
- **Yesterday's Low**: The bottom of the valley.
- **Yesterday's Close**: Where things settled at the final bell.

Plug those numbers into a formula (or let your charting software do the work), and BAM! You've got a set of CPR levels on your chart. These become your "watch zones" during today's trading.

Why the Heck Does CPR Matter?

Okay, it's not just lines on a chart. Here's why CPR zones are where things get interesting:

- **Trader Psychology:** We're creatures of habit. Lots of traders are eyeing yesterday's high/low, thinking, "If it bounces there again, I'm in!" This creates self-fulfilling prophecies—a ton of buy/sell orders concentrated around those CPR levels.
- **Big Players Love It:** Banks and hedge funds don't gamble. Their algorithms often factor in CPR levels, pushing the price action even harder around those zones.
- **Humans Like Obvious Stuff:** Even without knowing about CPR, people notice round numbers or yesterday's extremes. This naturally draws attention to CPR levels, adding even more fuel to the fire.

CPR Support, Resistance, and the Almighty Pivot Point

The most important CPR levels are:

- **CPR Support:** If prices dip here, bargain hunters swoop in, often creating bounces. Think of these as potential floors.
- **CPR Resistance:** When prices rise to these levels, sellers try to take profits, potentially stalling rallies.Think of them as ceilings.
- **The Pivot Point:** The king of CPR levels, calculated directly from high/low/close. This usually carries the most weight.

CPR in the Wild

Let's say stock XYZ had a high of $52, a low of $48, and closed at $50 yesterday. Our CPR calculations today might show us support at $49 and $48, with resistance at $51 and $52. Now, we watch:

- **Price drops close to $49 (potential CPR support)?** Get ready for bullish signals, a bounce could be brewing.
- **Price surges towards $51 (CPR resistance)?** Keep an eye out for sell-offs and bearish candlesticks.

WARNING: CPR Isn't a Crystal Ball

Here's the reality check:

- **Sometimes Prices Don't Care:** They'll blast right through CPR levels without blinking. That's why this is just ONE piece of our strategy.
- **Context is KING:** What works with CPR during a strong trend might fail miserably in a choppy market. We'll learn to adjust for this later.

Homework Time!

Before we move on, get hands-on:

- **Find a Chart:** Use Trading View (it's free) or whatever platform you like.
- **Play Detective:** Practice finding yesterday's high/low/close on some charts.
- **Observation Mode:** Watch how today's price interacts with yesterday's CPR zones. Do the bounces and reactions happen like we discussed?

Chart X-Ray: Deciphering Market Structure with the 20-EMA

In Chapter 1, we learned how CPR defines potential battle zones for today's trading session. But sometimes the battlefield itself shifts! That's where the 20-EMA comes in, helping us visualize the momentum and figure out whether those CPR zones are likely to hold or get blown right through.

The 20-EMA: Your Trend Detector

Here's the breakdown:

- **Price ABOVE a Rising 20-EMA:** Bulls likely have the upper hand. Expect prices to find support when they dip toward the EMA and treat it as a potential 'buy zone'.
- **Price BELOW a Falling 20-EMA:** Bears are in control. Rallies up into the falling EMA often become opportunities to short (sell), expecting a bounce-back down.
- **Flat (Sideways) 20-EMA:** Hold your horses! Market's unsure if it wants to go

up or down. Trade with caution, especially around those CPR levels.

Why Market Structure Matters

Knowing the trend does WAY more than just telling you "buy up, sell down":

- **Strength of CPR Levels:** A CPR resistance level gets a double whammy of resistance if it lines up with a falling 20-EMA during a downtrend. Conversely, strong uptrends make CPR support levels even more likely to hold when aided by a rising 20-EMA
- **Anticipating Breakouts:** When the price suddenly blasts through a powerful EMA (going from below to above a rising EMA, for example), it often signals a shift in sentiment...and those CPR levels from yesterday might not matter anymore!

20-EMA + CPR: The Dynamic Duo

Let's bring it back to stock XYZ:

- **Scenario 1:** CPR shows resistance at $51. BUT, price action is in a solid uptrend, trading above a rising 20-EMA. While $51 could still cause a stall, a decisive breakout through that CPR level (combined with continued buying strength) indicates that the bulls are taking charge.

- **Scenario 2:** CPR shows support at $49. Market's in a downtrend, with the price hugging below a falling 20-EMA. We watch $49 carefully, but if the bears have any steam left, they might take advantage of the weak market structure and punch straight through that CPR support.

Important Reminders

- **Trend, THEN Trade:** 20-EMA gives you the trend context, CPR levels help identify entry/exit zones within that trend.
- **No Indicator is Perfect:** Sometimes even the prettiest trend structures break down. Always manage your risk!
- **Zooming Out Helps:** Using the 20-EMA alongside a longer timeframe moving average (like the 50-period or 100-period SMA) is an extra layer to see if the short-term trend agrees with the bigger picture.

Homework Upgrade

- **Get That EMA On There:** Add the 20-period EMA to your charts. Analyze some historical price action alongside your CPR markings.
- **Trend Spotting Practice:** Find examples where price respects the 20-EMA as support or resistance during trends. Do these interactions line up with CPR levels?
- **Breakout Watch:** Look for examples where the price decisively busts through the 20-EMA. Did this result in a market structure change, invalidating existing CPR levels?

Next Time: Even with CPR and the EMA, we still need to figure out targets for taking profits and, more importantly, when to cut our losses short. That's what Chapter 3 is all about...

Support & Resistance: Your Multi-Timeframe Roadmap

CPR provides short-term battle zones, and the 20-EMA hints at which side might triumph. But markets have memories longer than a single trading day. That's where support and resistance (S&R) analysis shines, showing us landmarks traders will recall long after yesterday's CPR fades in relevance. Think of S&R as mountains and valleys on the price chart, respected across different timeframes.

What Exactly ARE Support and Resistance?

- **Support:** Like price floors. Areas where buyers historically step in, preventing the price from falling further (at least temporarily).
- **Resistance:** Think of them as ceilings. Places where sellers get excited to take profits, capping price rallies.

Why It Matters

- **Trader Psychology:** When a price approaches an area it struggled with before, people remember! Past support might attract fresh buyers even on smaller timeframes. The same goes for resistance that capped rallies before.

- **Turning Points:** Support levels that break often flip into future resistance (frustrated buyers get vengeful!). Likewise, when prices finally pierce through resistance, it might become the new support floor.
- **Targets & Risk Zones:** Strong S&R levels tell you both where to take profits AND where to place protective stop-losses.

S&R Across Timeframes: The Elephant Revealed

1. **Horizontal Lines: Zoom In, Zoom Out**
    - **Longer Timeframe:** On weekly or monthly charts, look for places where the price stalled repeatedly with decisive reversals. These are like mountains on the trading landscape, respected even during intraday action.
    - **Example:** Let's say stock XYZ has been trading in a wide range lately. On a monthly chart, you notice the price repeatedly found support near $40 and

bounced upwards several times. You also see $60 has acted as resistance during the last year. These key levels still hold relevance on your daily and even intraday charts!

- **Shorter Timeframe:** Smaller horizontal levels matter too! Significant highs/lows or round numbers from a few days back often translate into intraday S&R, especially when those lines align with CPR zones.

2. **Trendlines: Not Just For One Chart**

- **Bigger Picture:** Use daily or weekly charts to draw trendlines connecting significant highs or lows. These reveal underlying sentiment. Think of a weekly uptrend - even pullbacks within that trend attract buyers when short-term pullback lows approach your main trendline.
- **Example (Uptrend):** Stock ABC is in a bullish trend. Drawing a trendline connecting consecutive higher lows on a daily chart shows you the line of support bulls want to defend. Breaches

BELOW this line may signal a trend weakening.

- **Example (Downtrend):** Stock XYZ is in a weekly downtrend with lower highs. Connecting those highs reveals a clear resistance trendline bears keep enforcing. Breakouts ABOVE this signal potential trend shifts.
- **Intraday Tweaks:** Draw smaller timeframe trendlines for temporary, local market moves. Just remember the overall context of those bigger trendlines.

3. **Moving Averages: Timeframe Matching Matters!**
    - **Major Battlegrounds:** The 50-day, 100-day, or even 200-day SMA act as significant S&R areas on many timeframes. These take time to develop, reflecting strong trader sentiment behind them.

- **Example:** Stock EFG is known for volatility. Looking at a weekly chart, you see that the 100-day SMA has capped several major rallies and even provided support bounces in the past few months. Currently, the price is below the 100-SMA, signaling a bearish bias - even intraday rallies might get a colder reception near that longer-term MA.

- **Intraday Action:** Our fave, the 20-EMA, dynamically provides short-term S/R, but its power magnifies if it's aligning with a bigger-picture MA as well. A falling 20-EMA, while still acting as intraday resistance, is far riskier to short near when your daily chart also shows the 50-day SMA is sloping downwards.

4. **Fibonacci Levels: Math Gets Mystical (Optional)**

- For the advanced users! Fibonacci retracement tools highlight hidden S&R zones often watched by institutional traders (23.6%, 38.2%, 61.8%, etc.). After big, impulsive moves up or down, prices act like magnets pulling back toward these Fibonacci levels.

Homework Upgrade:

- **Zoom Out, Then In:** Pick a stock chart.
    - Weekly/Monthly - Find the dominant trend and major S&R zones it's been respecting for a while.
    - Daily - Zoom in to see if some of those larger-picture levels still hold relevance
    - Intraday (15min / 30min) - How do these major zones, combined with CPR, influence today's trading activity?

Trade Setups – Long Entries

We've learned to analyze the battlefield using CPR, spot the dominant trend with the 20-EMA, and locate those crucial support and resistance zones. Now, let's turn that knowledge into potential profitable trades! Remember, the magic of the "Tripod Strategy" lies in combining all three elements for the highest probability setups.

Your Long Trade Hunting Guide

1. **Trend Check:** Is the price in an uptrend (above the rising 20-EMA)? The stronger the trend, the better. Bonus points if it aligns with the direction on larger timeframes.
2. **Market Structure Check:** Is the overall market structure bullish? Look for higher highs and higher lows on your chosen timeframe. This will give your long trades a greater chance of success.
3. **Find the Floor:** Look for where the price is testing CPR support. Ideally, this aligns with a previous horizontal support level, a rising trendline, OR coincides with a

higher low within the bullish market structure. This offers even stronger confirmation.

4. **Breakout Watch (optional):** If the price is consolidating near CPR resistance, watch for a decisive break above with increased volume. This indicates buyers are finally overpowering sellers. Be extra cautious in downtrends or choppy market structure unless momentum has clearly shifted.
5. **EMA Bounce:** In strong uptrends, look for bullish candlestick patterns forming right on the rising 20-EMA. Ideally, you don't want long wicks below the EMA, which indicate failed breakdown attempts.
6. **Confirmation is Key:** Aligning these factors - trend, market structure, support, and potential breakout or bounce - boosts your trade's potential success.

Important Trade Management Reminders

- **Target Zones:** CPR levels often provide initial take-profit points. If momentum remains strong, look towards those bigger picture S&R resistances as the next price magnets.

- **Stop-Loss:** This is non-negotiable! Place your stop-loss below the key pivot zone your buy signal relied on. Breaking back below support (especially within Scenarios 3 or 5) invalidates the setup.

Homework Time

- **Backtest!:** Review old charts and focus on ONE entry type at a time. Did setups using CPR + S/R, aligned with bullish market structure lead to more successes compared to those without this confirmation?
- **Trend & Structure Hunt:** Analyze multiple timeframes to find stocks in strong uptrends right now, demonstrating clear higher highs and higher lows. Practice finding good "EMA Surf" entry zones along with potential breakout setups above key resistances.
- **Live Watchlist:** Choose a few stocks with clear patterns setting up at this very moment. Observe how they develop throughout the day, taking note of how their smaller price movements fit into the overall market structure

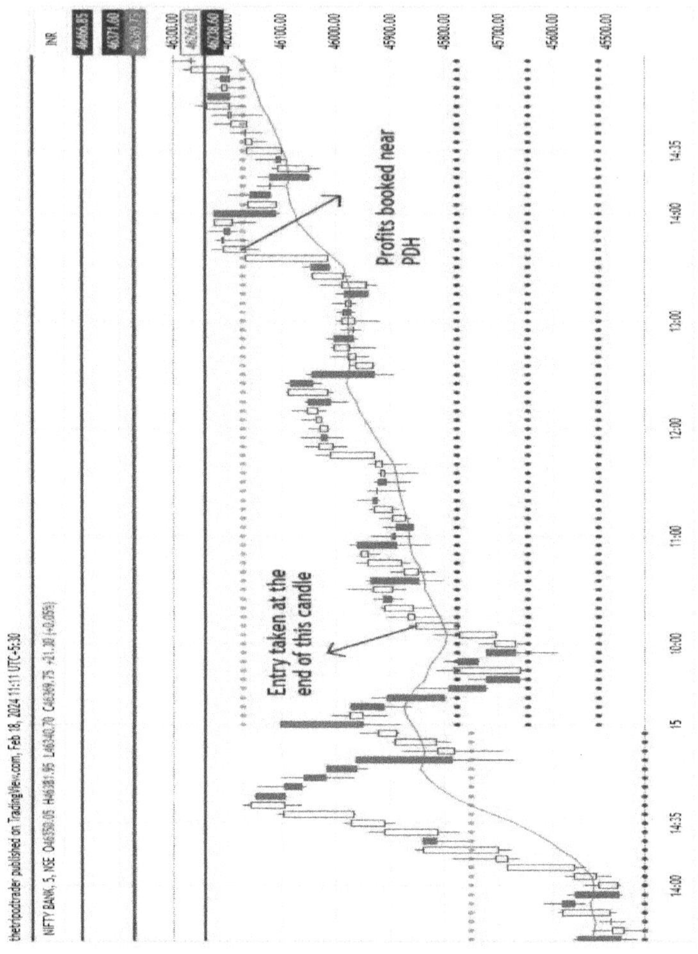
Entry taken at the end of this candle
Profits booked near PDH

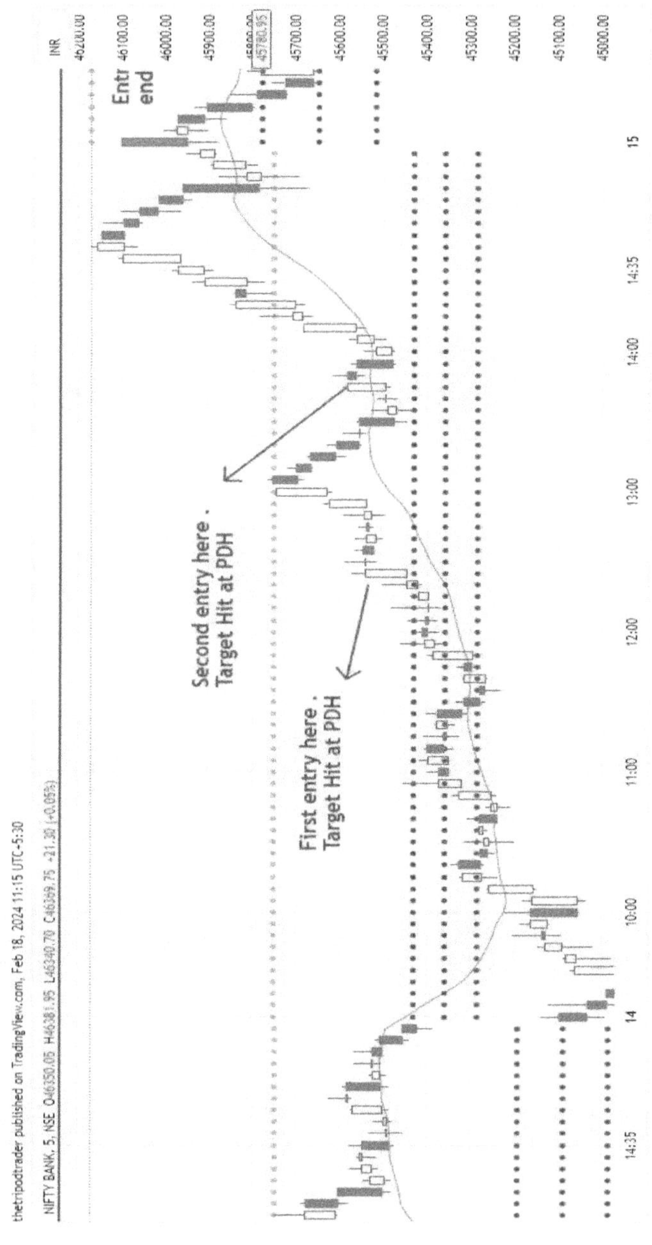
thetripodtrader published on TradingView.com, Feb 18, 2024 11:15 UTC-5:30
NIFTY BANK, 5, NSE O46350.05 H46381.95 L46340.70 C46369.75 +21.30 (+0.05%)
Second entry here . Target Hit at PDH
First entry here . Target Hit at PDH
Entr
end
INR
46100.00
46000.00
45900.00
45780.95
45700.00
45600.00
45500.00
45400.00
45300.00
45200.00
45100.00
45000.00
14:35
14
10:00
11:00
12:00
13:00
14:00
14:35
15
TradingView

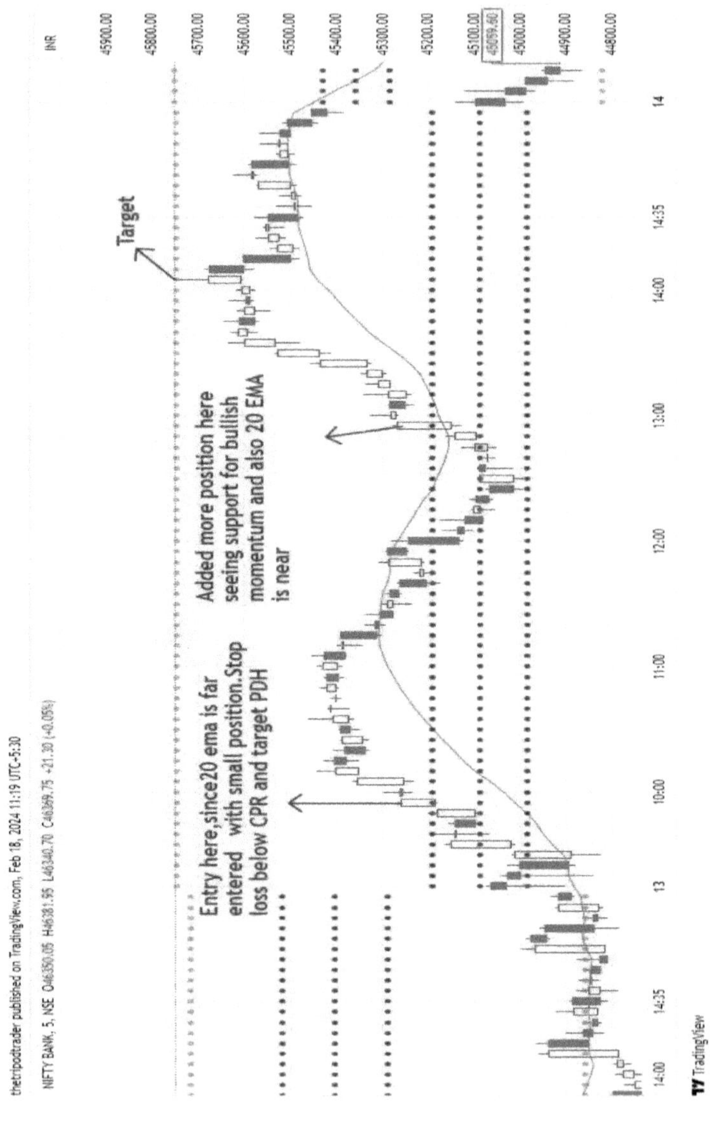
thetripodtrader published on TradingView.com, Feb 18, 2024 11:19 UTC+5:30
NIFTY BANK, 5, NSE O46350.05 H46381.95 L46340.70 C46369.75 +21.30 (+0.05%)
Target
Entry here,since20 ema is far entered with small position.Stop loss below CPR and target PDH
Added more position here seeing support for bullish momentum and also 20 EMA is near
TradingView

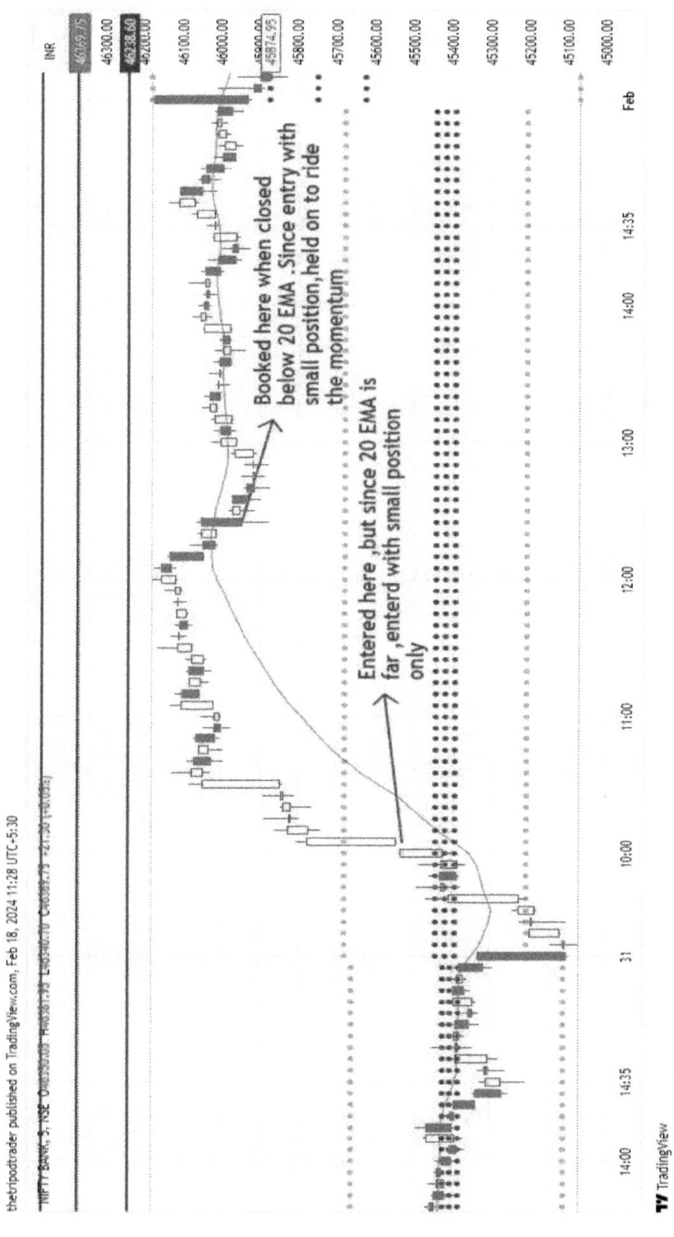
thetripodtrader published on TradingView.com, Feb 18, 2024 11:28 UTC-5:30
Booked here when closed below 20 EMA .Since entry with small position,held on to ride the momentum
Entered here ,but since 20 EMA is far ,enterd with small position only
INR
45874.95
46100.00
46000.00
45800.00
45700.00
45600.00
45500.00
45400.00
45300.00
45200.00
45100.00
45000.00
14:00
14:35
31
10:00
11:00
12:00
13:00
14:00
14:35
Feb
TradingView

Trade Setups - Short Entries

We've covered how to spot promising long trades (buying low, selling high), but what about when the market's headed south? Understanding how to short can add powerful versatility to your trading toolkit. Let's break down how to find those high-probability short entries.

The "Tripod Strategy" for Shorting

Remember how CPR, trend, and support/resistance analysis guide our long trades? The same concepts apply in reverse for shorts:

1. **Spot the Downtrend:** A falling price below the 20-EMA is your first clue. Ideally, this downtrend aligns with what you see on larger timeframes (daily, weekly).
2. **Bearish Structure:** Is the market making lower highs and lower lows? Shorting within a clear downtrend gives your trade the best chance of success.
3. **Hitting the Ceiling:** Price testing CPR resistance is a key zone to watch. This resistance ideally lines up with previous

resistance, a trendline, OR forms a lower high within the bearish structure.

4. **The Breakdown:** If price gets stuck near CPR support, look for it to break BELOW decisively with increased volume. This shows sellers getting the upper hand. Be extra cautious shorting against the trend (during an uptrend), unless momentum clearly changes sides.
5. **The EMA Reject:** Strong downtrends often see price bounce off the falling 20-EMA. Look for bearish candles forming right on the EMA, without long wicks above (which signal failed rallies).

Key Reminders:

- **Managing Targets:** Use CPR levels to set initial profit targets, then reassess and aim for larger support zones if momentum stays strong.
- **Stop-Losses are Sacred:** ALWAYS place your stop-loss above the pivot point where your short signal formed. A break back up suggests you got this one wrong!

Practice Time!

- **Backtest Scenarios:** Try this on old charts. Did combining CPR and S/R with those trend filters help identify good shorting opportunities?
- **Downtrend Hunt:** Use tools to identify stocks in clear downtrends with distinct lower highs and lower lows. Practice spotting "EMA Reject" zones and areas where prices might break down further.
- **Create a Live Watchlist:** Pick a few stocks with bearish setups right now. See how they play out over the day.

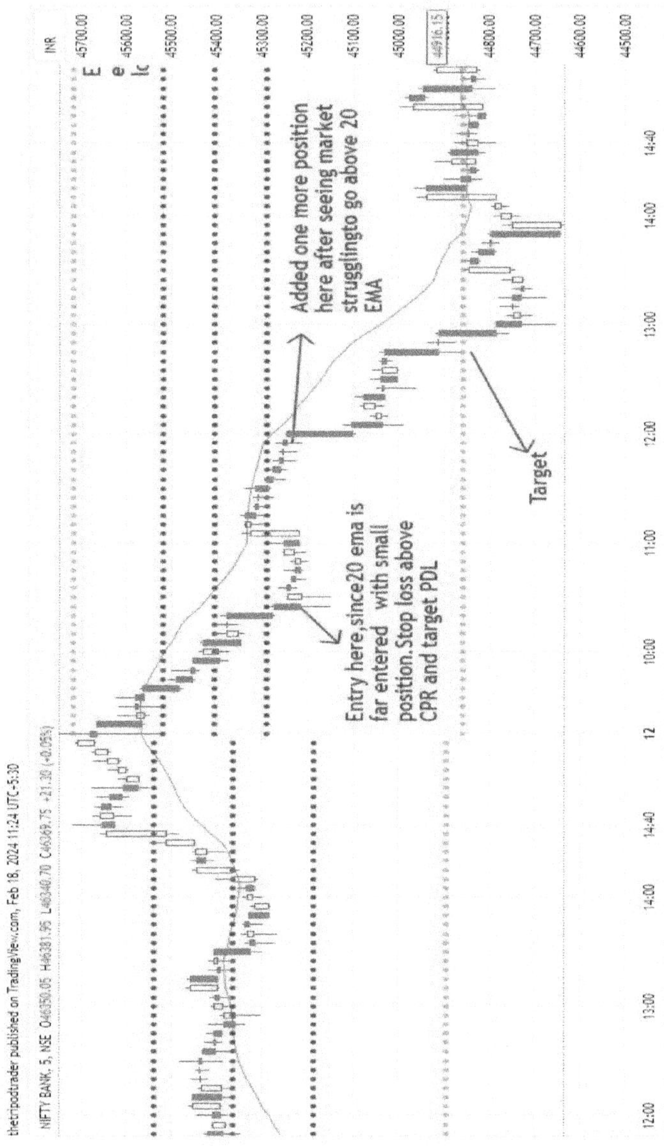
thetripodtrader published on TradingView.com, Feb 18, 2024 11:24 UTC-5:30
NIFTY BANK, 5, NSE O46350.05 H46381.95 L46340.70 C46369.75 +21.30 (+0.05%)
Entry here,since20 ema is far entered with small position.Stop loss above CPR and target PDL
Added one more position here after seeing market strugglingto go above 20 EMA
Target
INR
45700.00
45600.00
45500.00
45400.00
45300.00
45200.00
45100.00
45000.00
44916.15
44800.00
44700.00
44600.00
44500.00
12:00
13:00
14:00
14:40
12
10:00
11:00
12:00
13:00
14:00
14:40
TradingView

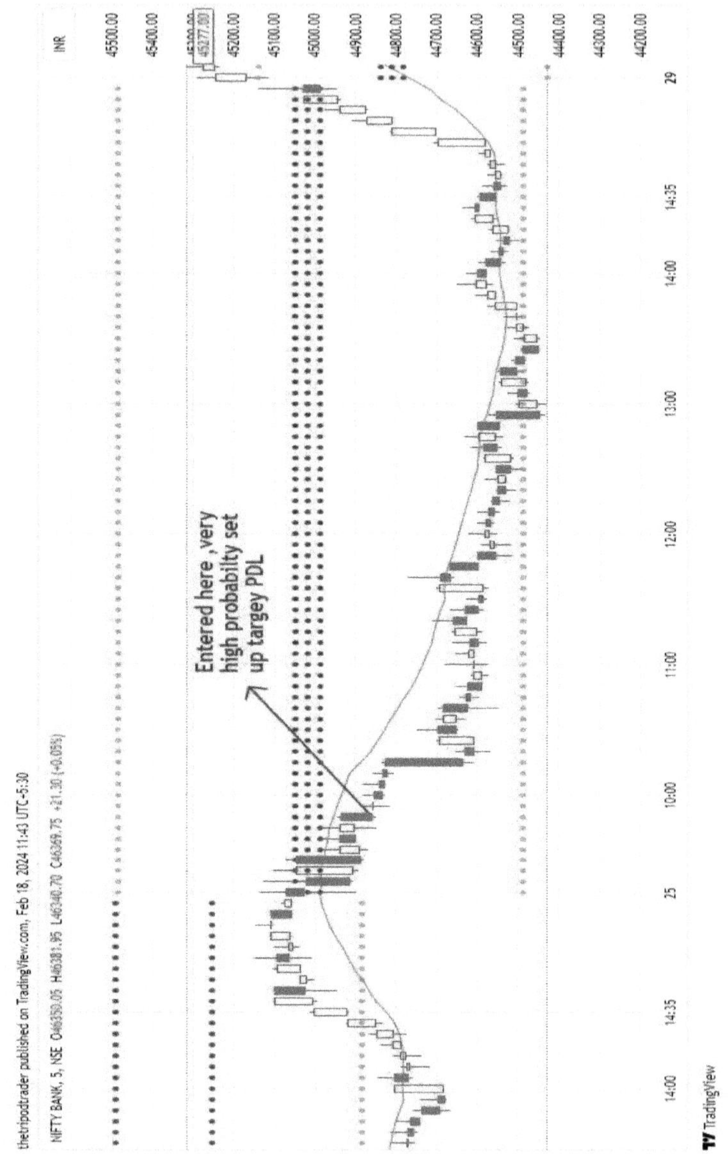
thetripodtrader published on TradingView.com, Feb 18, 2024 11:43 UTC-5:30
Entered here ,very high probabilty set up targey PDL
TradingView

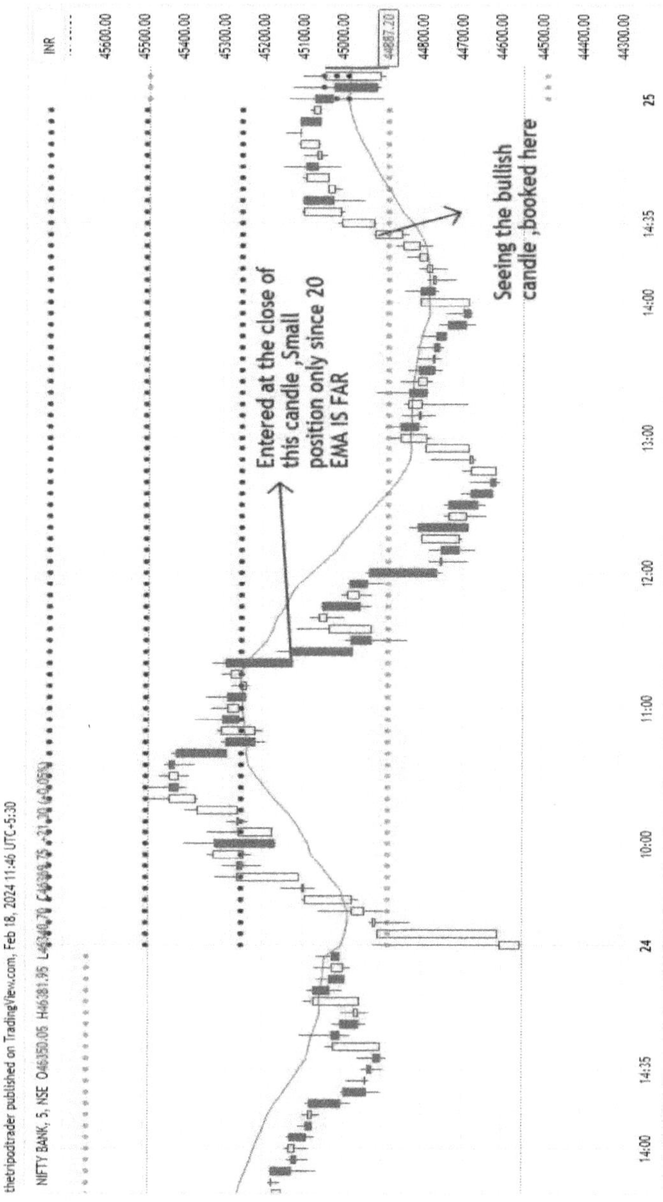
thetripodtrader published on TradingView.com, Feb 18, 2024 11:46 UTC+5:30
Entered at the close of this candle ,Small position only since 20 EMA IS FAR
Seeing the bullish candle ,booked here
TradingView

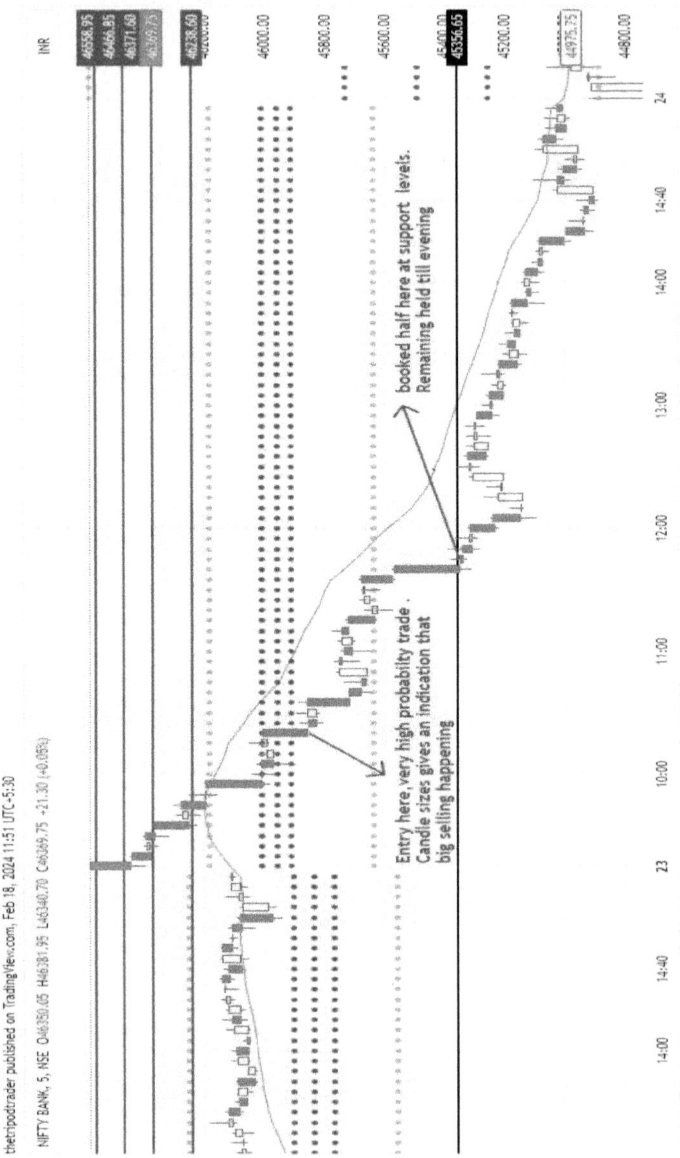
thetripodtrader published on TradingView.com, Feb 18, 2024 11:51 UTC+5:30
NIFTY BANK, 5, NSE O46350.05 H46381.95 L46340.70 C46369.75 +21.30 (+0.05%)
Entry here, very high probability trade . Candle sizes gives an indication that big selling happening
booked half here at support levels. Remaining held till evening
TradingView

"No Trade" Days – When the Tripod Wobbles

The Tripod Strategy thrives on aligning trend strength, CPR zones, and clear support/resistance levels. However, the market doesn't always offer textbook setups. Understanding when to abstain from trading is just as crucial as recognizing high-probability entries. Here's how to spot those potentially tricky "no trade" days:

Scenario 1: The Trend is Missing

- **EMA Indecision:** The price is hovering around the 20-EMA, lacking directional conviction. It might be crossing above and below repeatedly. Stay clear until a clearer trend develops.
- **Market Structure Chaos:** No distinct higher highs/lower lows on your chart. Instead, there's sideways chop or seemingly random peaks and valleys.
- **Conflicting Timeframes:** Your main timeframe might suggest a slight downtrend, but the larger timeframe

paints a picture of consolidation or an uptrend. It's best to wait for alignment.

Scenario 2: CPR Confusion

- **Wide CPR Range:** The difference between yesterday's high, low, and close is unusually large. This suggests high volatility and unpredictability, increasing the uncertainty of where support/resistance might lie today.
- **No Reliable Overlap:** CPR levels (especially resistance for shorts and support for longs) don't clearly align with other key price zones like past horizontal support/resistance or trendlines. When CPR stands alone, its power weakens.

Scenario 3: Weak Signals, Conflicting Market

- **Indecisive Candlesticks:** Even near your potential entry zones, doji candles, candles with long wicks on both sides, and other patterns signal a tug-of-war between buyers and sellers.
- **Counter-Trend Signals:** You see a potential EMA bounce for a long trade, but the larger timeframe is in a strong

downtrend. Trying to catch a falling knife often gets you cut!

- **Major News/Earnings**: High-impact announcements can shake up markets unexpectedly. It's often wise to sit out volatile periods, especially until you see the initial price reaction play out.

The Importance of Patience

- **Forced Trades Lead to Mistakes:** Jumping into a trade just to trade is a recipe for losses. Wait for the market to give you those solid Tripod setups.
- **Capital preservation is Key:** If a day lacks clear setups, avoid taking unnecessary risks. Preserve your trading capital for the high-probability opportunities that always come along.
- **"No Trade" Days Build Discipline:** The best traders know when to be active and when to stay patient. Mastering this discipline brings long-term success.

Practice Makes Perfect!

- **Backtest:** Look at a wide variety of charts and specifically hunt for days where the Tripod wouldn't work well. Ask yourself "Could I have spotted this lack of clarity early?".
- **Journal:** When considering a trade, write down WHY you think it's a strong setup. If you find yourself struggling to provide evidence for a trade, that's often a sign to skip it.
- **Paper Trading:** Test out your "no trade" day assessment in real-time with paper trading or a simulator. See if your instincts for staying sidelined save you from losses.

- 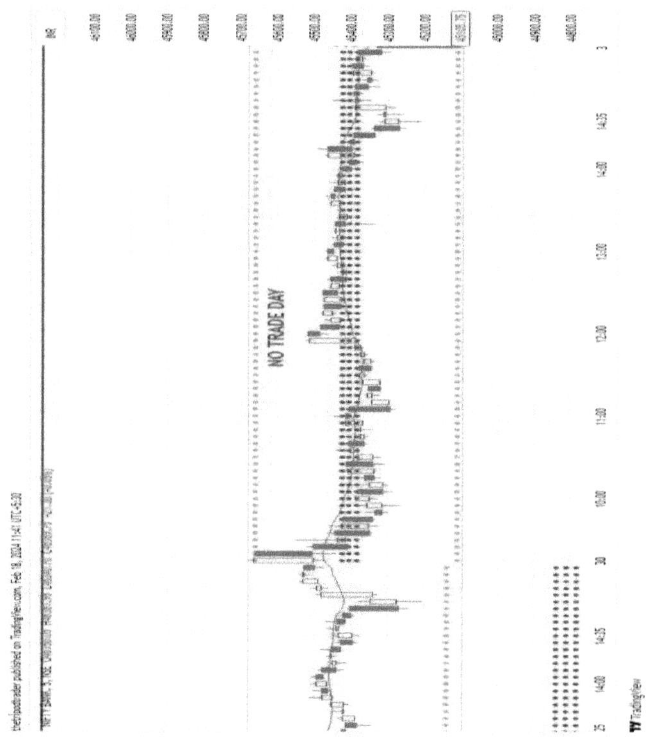
NO TRADE DAY

•

thetripodtrader published on TradingView.com, Feb 18, 2024 12:00 UTC+5:30
NIFTY BANK, 5, NSE O46350.05 H46381.95 L46340.70 C46369.75 +21.30 (+0.05%)
INR
47800.00
47700.00
47600.00
47506.70
47400.00
47300.00
47200.00
47100.00
NO TRADE DAY
13:00
14:00
14:40
11
10:00
11:00
12:00
13:00
14:00
14:40
TradingView

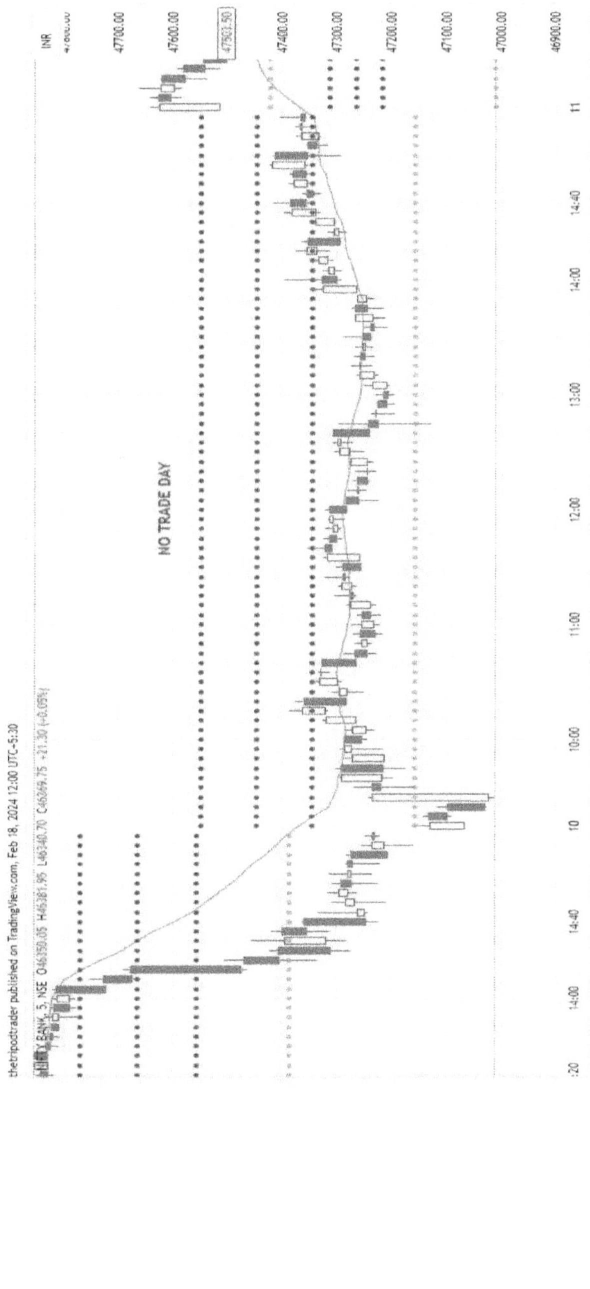
thetripodtrader published on TradingView.com, Feb 18, 2024 12:00 UTC+5:30
BANK, 5, NSE
NO TRADE DAY
INR
47700.00
47600.00
47503.50
47400.00
47300.00
47200.00
47100.00
47000.00
46900.00
14:00
14:40
10
10:00
11:00
12:00
13:00
14:00
14:40
11
TradingView

Risk: The Heart of the Tripod Strategy

Let's face it, trading is inherently risky. But within the Tripod Strategy, every risk becomes manageable when you have the guts to tackle it head-on. To navigate the unpredictable market waters, smart risk management is essential. This means mastering not only your risk-reward ratio but also factoring in the overall probability of a successful trade.

Understanding the Risk-Reward Ratio

This simple but powerful concept is about weighing the potential reward of a trade against the potential loss. To calculate it, divide your potential profit by your potential loss.

Let's say you identify a trade with a potential profit of $500. Your well-placed stop-loss (more on that soon!) limits your downside to $250. Bingo! You're looking at a solid 2:1 risk-reward ratio - for every dollar you risk, you could make two back.

Why the Tripod Strategy Loves Risk-Reward (and Probability!)

Here's why these principles are cornerstones of the Tripod Strategy:

- **Capital Protection:** A few bad trades can sink your account if you're not careful. With a good risk-reward ratio, you limit your losses and preserve your trading capital.
- **Maximizing Profits:** It might seem backward, but when you focus on trades with higher potential rewards, it creates the possibility of being wrong more often than right but still turning a consistent profit!
- **Mental Clarity:** Knowing your maximum loss beforehand eliminates the panic-driven decision-making that can sabotage your gains.
- **Assessing Confidence:** The Tripod Strategy provides clear signals. The more your three constituents (fundamentals,

technicals, and sentiment) align, the higher the probability of success in a trade.

The Tripod Strategy with Position Sizing

Let's take this to the next level:

- **Know Your Limit (Stop-Loss):** Before entering a trade, set a non-negotiable stop-loss price. This is your exit point to prevent small losses from spiraling out of control.
- **Aim High (Profit Target):** Use your technical analysis skills to pinpoint a likely exit price where you can bank your gains.
- **Do the Math:** Divide your potential profit by your potential loss. With the Tripod Strategy, aim for ratios of 2:1 or even better.
- **Confidence = Size:** If all three Tripod constituents signal a strong buy, consider taking a larger position. If there's less alignment, reduce your trade size to reflect the higher uncertainty.
- **Discipline is Key:** Don't fall for any trade that looks halfway decent. If it doesn't fit

your risk-reward criteria AND align with your Tripod signals, resist the temptation and move on.

Example Time

Consider two trades fitting the Tripod mold:

- **High Confidence Trade**
  - 1:3 Risk-Reward
  - Entry Price: $50
  - Stop-Loss: $45 (Risking $5)
  - Profit Target: $65 (Potential $15 gain)
  - All Tripod factors pointing towards a buy = larger position size
- **Uncertain Trade**
  - 1:2 Risk-Reward
  - Entry Price: $50
  - Stop-Loss: $45 (Risking $5)
  - Profit Target: $55 (Potential $5 gain)
  - Mixed Tripod signals = smaller position size

The Tripod Takeaway

While the Risk-Reward ratio helps you analyze individual trades, adding the layer of confidence assessment and position sizing transforms it into a holistic risk management tool. This approach protects your capital and amplifies your profits when conditions are in your favor, setting you apart as a truly skillful trader.

Back testing & Tweaking: Leveling Up Your Tripod Strategy

So, you've got the Tripod basics - spotting trends, CPRs, all that good stuff. But before throwing real money at it, how do you KNOW it'll shine for YOUR trading style? Enter: backtesting and optimization. Think of it like target practice before the big game.

Why Backtesting is Your Trading Buddy

- **History Repeats Itself...Kinda:** Backtesting lets you replay past charts, seeing how your strategy would have done. Not magic, but helps spot holes or surprising strengths.
- **Find Your Timeframe Sweet Spot:** Tripod work great on daily charts, but maybe YOU kill it on 4-hour? Testing tells you, not guesswork.
- **CPR Experimentation:** Does yesterday's close, open, or something fancier give the strongest support/resistance on your fave stocks? Backtest to find out!

Optimization: Small Tweaks, Big Potential

- **One Thing at a Time:** Ditch the kitchen-sink approach. Test adding just ONE filter, or a tighter stop-loss, and see the impact before changing everything.
- **Don't Chase Perfection:** Winning every single "past" trade is misleading. Look for what CONSISTENTLY makes the biggest difference.
- **Test Across Chaos:** Gotta see how the strategy holds up on good days, bad days, and sideways messes. Don't fall for strategies that only work in your ideal perfect world.

Extras to Consider

- **Newsflash!:** Big surprise news messed up a winning trade? Note that when replaying, it wouldn't have been predictable even using the strategy perfectly.
- **Trade Diary + Replay = Growth:** Did you make some impulsive, non-Tripod decisions when looking at past charts? Be honest! Awareness is half the battle.

Here's a Tasty Example

Let's say 60% of your losses hit stop-losses that were WAY far away from the entry. Could going slightly tighter actually give trades breathing room and improve your profits? This is what you'd investigate!

Important Caveats

- **Start Simple, Get Smart:** Optimization gets real tricky if you haven't nailed the basics yet.
- **Paper Trading FTW:** After adjusting, trade without real money for a bit. Testing beats blindly trusting even the best backtests.

Backtesting and optimization are how you become a more strategic trader. It unveils hidden weaknesses, highlights your strengths, and lets you personalize a strategy that's tailored to you. And that's WAY more powerful than trying to copy-paste someone else's setup.

Your Secret Weapon – Journaling for Strategy & Mindset Mastery

The Tripod Strategy provides your trading framework, but a detailed journal reveals what's going on inside your head while you apply it. Think of it like an athlete reviewing game footage: painful to watch sometimes, but the fastest way to identify where gains can be made.

Why Write Things Down?

- **Your Brain Lies to You:** We misremember bad decisions, gloss over wins we got lucky on, and invent reasons where none existed. A journal combats this treacherous optimism.
- **Patterns Emerge:** Were you consistently taking trades too early when feeling impatient? Do Mondays make you overconfident? Seeing it laid out gets you closer to solutions.
- **Tripod Spotlights:** Did a setup technically fit your rules, but you hesitated with an underlying gut feeling? That instinct might be worth honing on future setups.

What to Log (Sample)

- **Market Details:** Date/time, symbol traded, brief notes on overall market context (volatile day, bullish news, etc.)
- **The Trade Idea:** Trend direction, CPR levels justifying setup, your planned stop-loss and initial target.
- **Pre-Trade Mindset:** Stressed? Bored? Confident? A one-word emotion check-in reveals A LOT later
- **The Execution:** Did you trade exactly as planned? Any hesitations or rule-breaking to note.
- **Trade Outcome:** Win/Loss is less important than WHY. Luck? Discipline? Or did the Tripod fail completely?

Reviewing for Growth

- **Look for Repetition:** Multiple trades ruined by FOMO? This isn't about beating yourself up, it's about seeing red flags BEFORE they damage your account.
- **Honesty Over Harshness:** You'll make mistakes; the journaling goal is progress, not punishment. Identifying errors lets you devise safeguards moving forward.

- **Tripod Tweaks:** Maybe the strategy requires adjustment for your personality. Should targets be smaller to reduce emotional blowback when they're hit? This awareness improves the strategy itself.

Extra Journaling Power-Ups

- **Screenshots:** Include charts WITH your trade setup drawn in. Sometimes the mistake only becomes obvious visually.
- **Video Journal Alternative:** Struggle with writing? Record yourself talking through trade ideas before you click "buy/sell". Awkward for sure, but revealing about subconscious thinking.
- **Combine with Backtesting:** Noticed fear driving decisions during replay? Now your backtesting has additional angles to focus on.

Key Takeaways

- **Consistency Pays Off:** Daily journaling, even short entries, is more useful than marathon sessions once a month. Habits beat heroic effort.
- **It's NOT All About Trades:** Did you skip proper research due to burnout, or cut a

loser early out of panic? Your overall well-being impacts your trading too.

- **There's No "Right" Way:** Find the methods that force YOU to look critically at your trading actions and the thoughts behind them.

Conquering Obstacles: Navigating False Breakouts, Emotions, and More

The world of trading is fraught with obstacles that can derail even the most disciplined investor. Understanding and overcoming these challenges is essential for sustained success. The Tripod Strategy, while powerful, is not immune to the volatility of the markets. In this chapter, we'll delve into strategies for handling hurdles specifically associated with this approach.

Common Pitfalls Encountered with the Tripod Strategy

- **False Breakouts:** Breakouts are a significant component of the Tripod Strategy, but premature action on a false signal can lead to losses. A price may seem to break out of a pattern but quickly reverse, resulting in a whipsawing effect. These traps can shake confidence and make traders hesitant to act on future, genuine breakouts.
- **Overtrading:** Periods of market consolidation or choppy activity can tempt traders to try and force profitable

scenarios. Overtrading in these conditions is especially perilous with the Tripod Strategy, where clear technical signals are crucial. This tendency can result in increased commissions and sub-optimal entry and exit points.

Recognizing Emotional Triggers and Developing Techniques to Manage Them

Trading and investing are inherently emotional affairs. Fear, greed, and impulsiveness can lead to irrational decisions. Key aspects of mastering your emotions include:

- **Self-Awareness:** Recognize the emotional triggers that influence your behavior. Do losses drive you towards revenge trading? Does a period of high profitability leave you feeling overly confident? Identifying these patterns is the first step in managing them.
- **Mindfulness:** Practices like deep breathing and meditation can help bring calmness to the trading process. Taking brief breaks away from the screen when emotions start to run high can make a major difference.

- **Trading Journal:** Documenting your trades, including the reason for entry, exit, and your emotional state throughout, can shed light on unhealthy patterns. Review it to identify where emotions cloud your judgment and lead to mistakes.

Strategies for Handling False Breakouts and Minimizing Their Impact

- **Confirmation:** Employ tools like volume analysis or multiple timeframes to increase the reliability of signals, helping to weed out false breakouts.
- **Patience:** It's critical to wait for a true breakout to be confirmed. Jumping the gun based on premature assumptions can be costly.
- **Strict Stop-Losses:** Stops protect your capital on trades that turn unfavorable. Utilizing disciplined stop-loss orders helps minimize the impact of false breakouts.

Developing Mental Resilience in the Face of Losses

Losses are inevitable in trading. Building mental resilience to handle them can significantly improve long-term outcomes:

- **Risk Management:** Trade with a clearly defined risk per trade, never risking more than you're comfortable losing. This prevents single trades from spiraling into catastrophic losses.
- **Expect Drawdowns:** Accept that temporary drawdowns are an inherent part of trading. Mentally preparing for them makes it easier to stick to your strategy during unfavorable periods.
- **Learning Mindset:** Analyze losing trades dispassionately. Focus on recognizing where errors were made and extract lessons to refine your approach, enhancing future strategies.

Remember: Successful trading is about developing skills to address market-related hurdles as well as overcoming your internal ones. Combining technical precision with emotional control will give you an edge to navigate the challenges of the markets and strive for success.

Essential Tripod Trading Rules & Mastering Your Mindset

The Tripod Strategy offers your framework, but unwavering discipline and strategic execution make the difference between theory and profit. These rules enhance your Tripod analysis and forge the crucial mindset to stay in the game for long-term success.

Foundation Pillars

1. **Rules Are Your Ruler:** The strategy, your pre-defined risk limits, and trading plan provide structure. When violated, step back and reassess.
2. **Patience Pays:** Wait for candle closes at critical levels, never force trades, and use "no trade" days strategically for observation and learning.
3. **Risk Before Reward:** Position sizing reflects setup strength (stronger = possibly larger, weaker = smaller). Know your non-negotiable stop-loss BEFORE placing an order.

4. **Structure is Supreme:** Analyze the bigger picture using multiple timeframes. Does the overall market context support your planned short or long trade? Fight against, not with, the dominant flow.

5. **Tripod Purity:** Master the core concepts of trend, CPR, and support/resistance before adding unnecessary complexity. Too many indicators slow your decisions.

6. **Partial Profit Protection:** Book some gains near previous swing highs/lows - these act as temporary barriers. Take money off the table while staying active.

7. **Adaptive Risk Management:** Learn the art of trailing stops for some flexibility but avoid being shaken out by normal volatility. Wide, fixed stops limit your potential.

8. **Winners Need Space (Sometimes):** If a trade breaks significant levels with momentum and maintains strong Tripod signals, it may be profitable to ride a portion longer, protecting profits on the rest.

9. **News = Volatility:** High-impact events derail setups. Consider profit preservation

BEFORE surprises happen, or adjust position sizing if you anticipate wild swings.

10. **The Critical Filter:** Impulsive moves often stem from impatience and greed. Ask: Does this trade TRULY meet my core Tripod criteria, or am I succumbing to emotion?
11. **Lessons in Losses:** Analyze losing trades objectively. Are there recurring weaknesses in your strategy or emotional blindspots? Great traders evolve after mistakes.
12. **Don't Feed the Greed Monster:** Use targets, partial profit-taking, and discipline to combat unrealistic goals. Giving back profits is demoralizing and counterproductive.
13. **Stay Alert on Mondays:** Weekend excitement can create over-eagerness at the week's open. Be especially mindful of impulsive trading during this time.
14. **Honest Foundation:** Success requires brutal self-assessment. Identify

weaknesses, seek improvement, and ditch your ego at the door.

15. **Your Instruments, Your Strengths:** Focus on understanding a handful of markets or assets in depth for the best edge.
16. **Adapt or Get Left Behind:** Market conditions change; can your strategy and mindset adjust, or is it best to sit out until conditions suit it?
17. **Buffer for Unknowns:** Unexpected life events happen. Ensure you have some cash cushion outside your actively traded capital to protect your trading journey.
18. **Scaling Up Too Fast**-Early wins tempt larger trades without earned confidence. One bad outcome destroys gains and confidence. Start small, scale-up systematically based on proven performance.
19. **Continuous Improvement**-Markets, your skills – always evolve. Analyze past trading, seek new concepts, test Tripod optimizations on historical data to stay ahead

20. **Don't Try to Outsmart the Market**- Forcing low-odds setups, expecting your genius overtakes the market - you'll lose. Stick religiously to your clear Tripod criteria; no setup, no trade.

Marked Charts

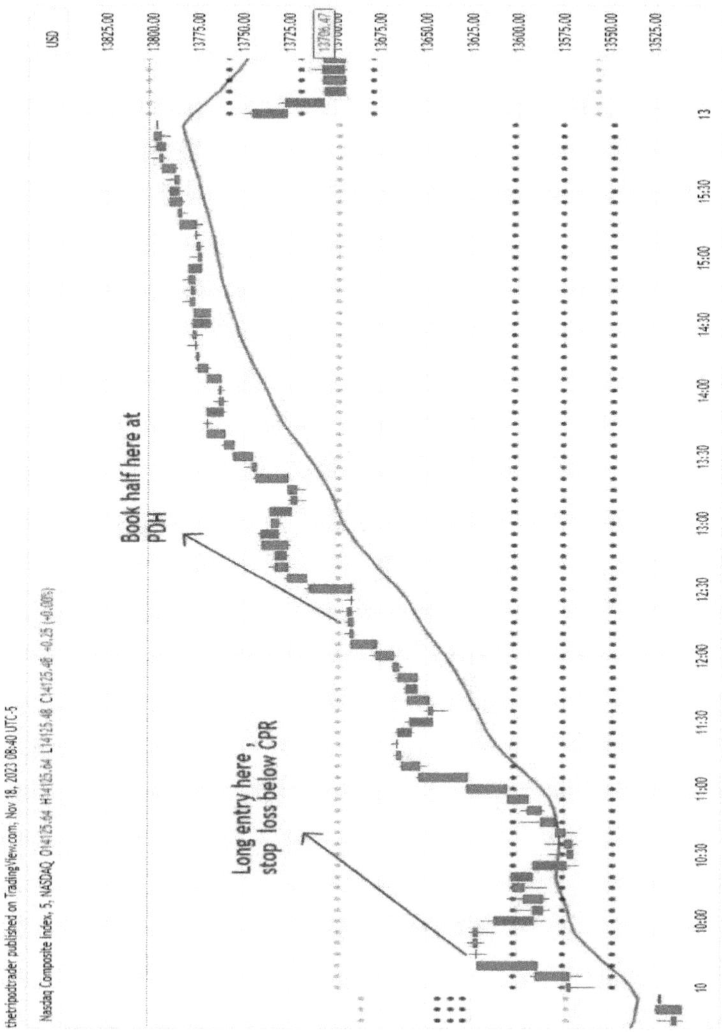

thetripodtrader published on TradingView.com, Nov 18, 2023 08:49 UTC-5
Nasdaq Composite Index, 5, NASDAQ O14125.64 H14125.64 L14125.48 C14125.48 +0.25 (+0.00%)
USD
Third entry here.
Half booked at PDL
and remaining at end
of day
Second entry here.
Booked at PDH since
market is volatile
First entry here .
Stop loss hit
13740.00
13720.00
13700.00
13680.00
13660.00
13640.00
13620.00
13602.36
13580.00
13560.00
13540.00
13520.00
13500.00
13480.00
15:00
9
10:10
11:00
12:00
13:00
14:00
15:00
10
10:10
TradingView

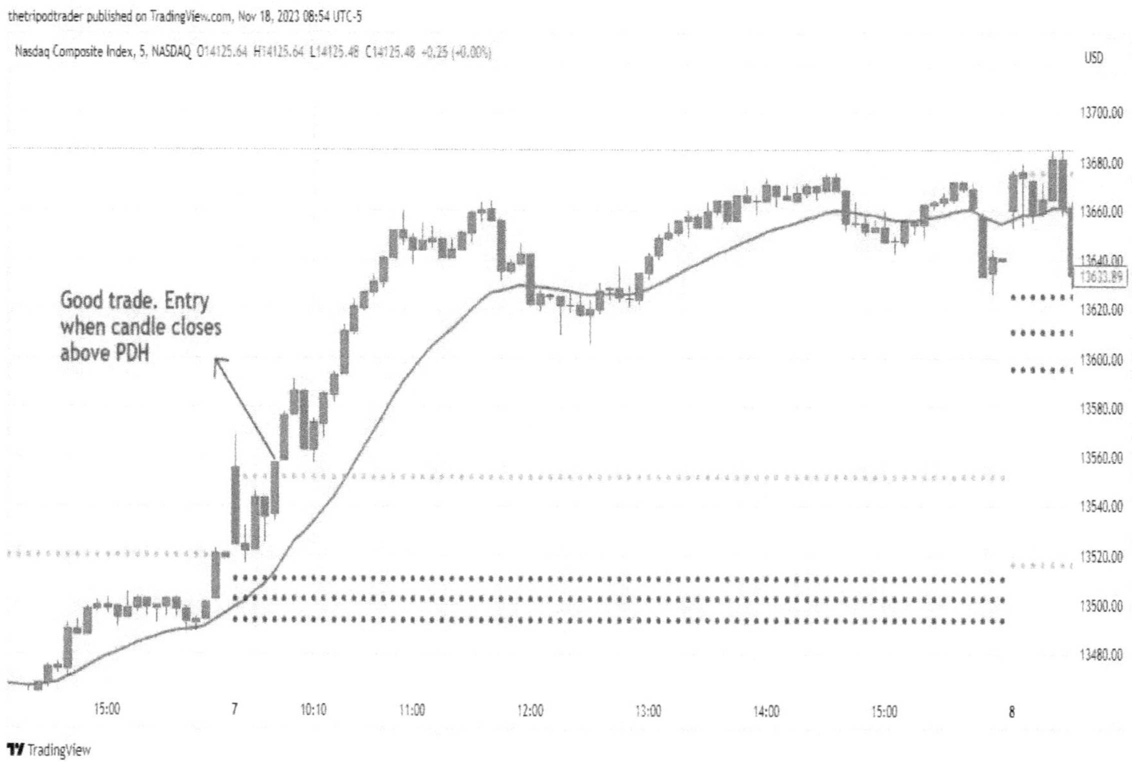

thetripodtrader published on TradingView.com, Nov 18, 2023 08:54 UTC-5
Nasdaq Composite Index, 5, NASDAQ O14125.64 H14125.64 L14125.48 C14125.48 -0.25 (-0.00%)
USD
13700.00
13680.00
13660.00
13640.00
13633.89
13620.00
13600.00
13580.00
13560.00
13540.00
13520.00
13500.00
13480.00
15:00
7
10:10
11:00
12:00
13:00
14:00
15:00
8
Good trade. Entry when candle closes above PDH
TradingView

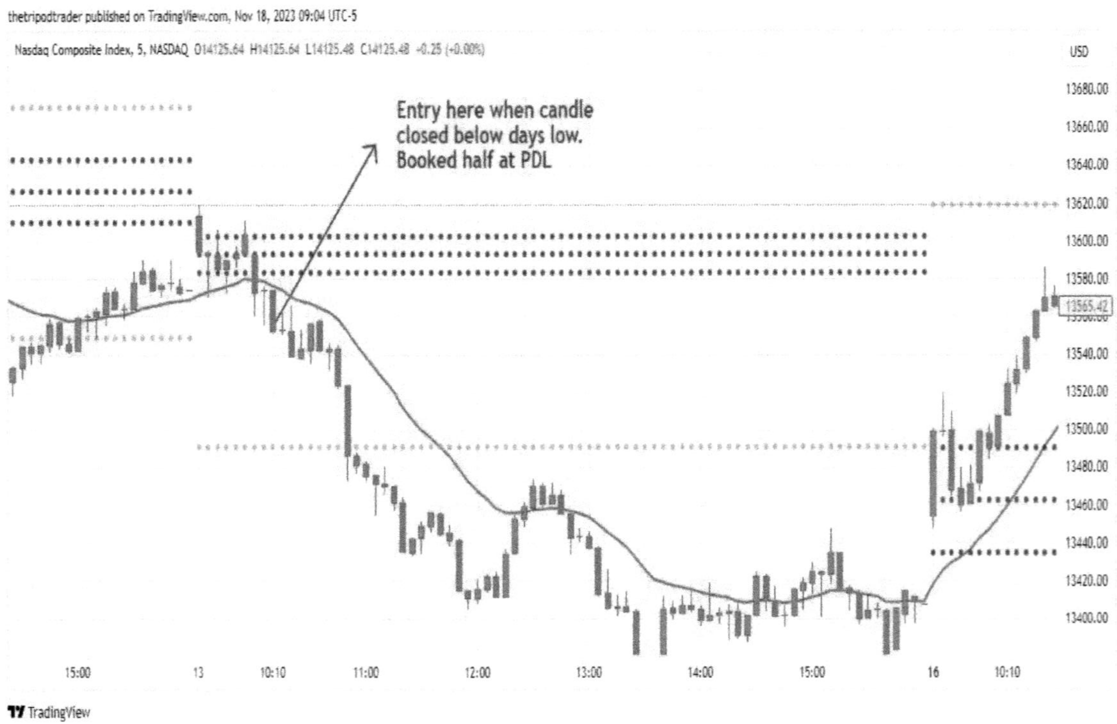
thetripodtrader published on TradingView.com, Nov 18, 2023 09:04 UTC-5
Nasdaq Composite Index, 5, NASDAQ O14125.64 H14125.64 L14125.48 C14125.48 -0.25 (+0.00%)
USD
13680.00
13660.00
13640.00
13620.00
13600.00
13580.00
13565.42
13540.00
13520.00
13500.00
13480.00
13460.00
13440.00
13420.00
13400.00
Entry here when candle
closed below days low.
Booked half at PDL
15:00
13
10:10
11:00
12:00
13:00
14:00
15:00
16
10:10
TradingView

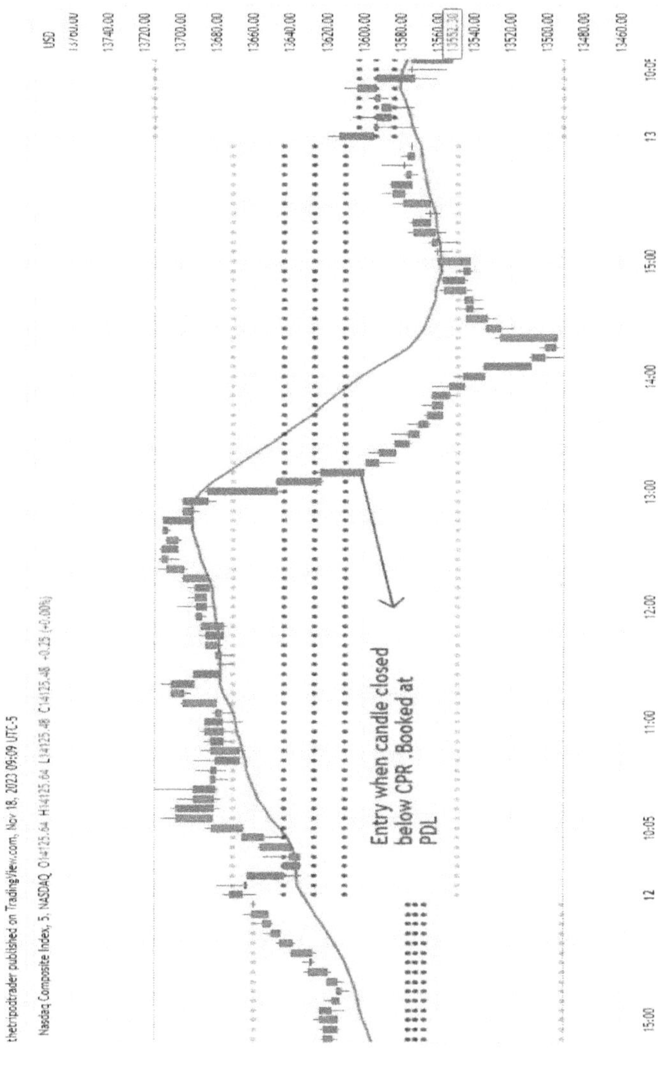
thetripodtrader published on TradingView.com, Nov 18, 2023 09:09 UTC-5
Nasdaq Composite Index, 5, NASDAQ
Entry when candle closed below CPR .Booked at PDL
TradingView

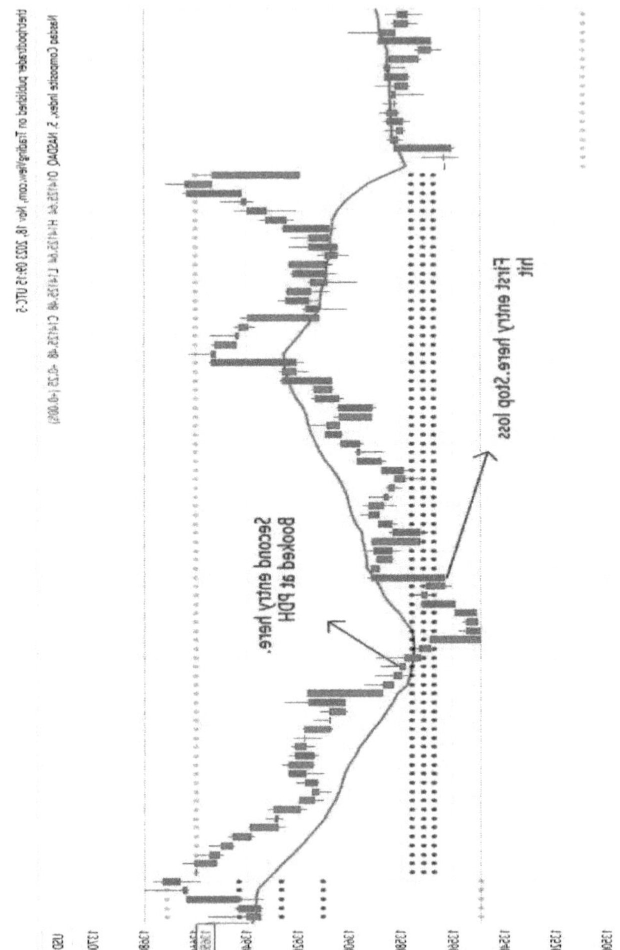
First entry here.Stop loss hit
Second entry here. Booked at PDH
TradingView

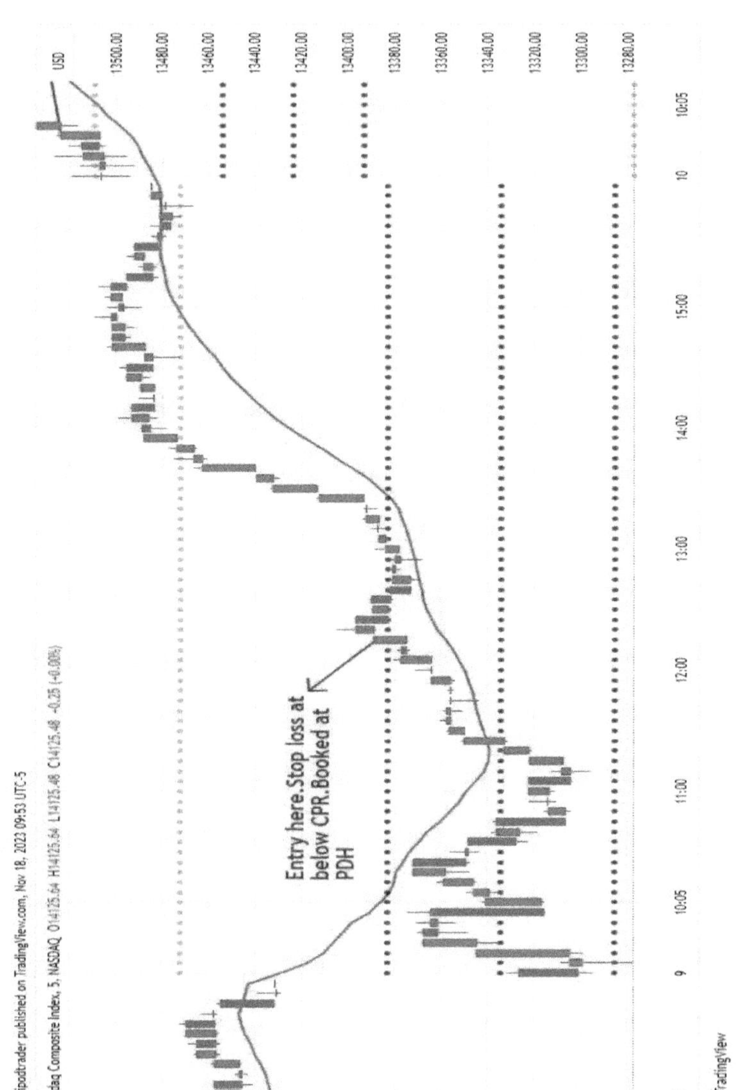
thetripodtrader published on TradingView.com, Nov 18, 2023 09:53 UTC-5
Nasdaq Composite Index, 5, NASDAQ O14125.64 H14125.64 L14125.48 C14125.48 −0.25 (−0.00%)
Entry here.Stop loss at below CPR.Booked at PDH
TradingView

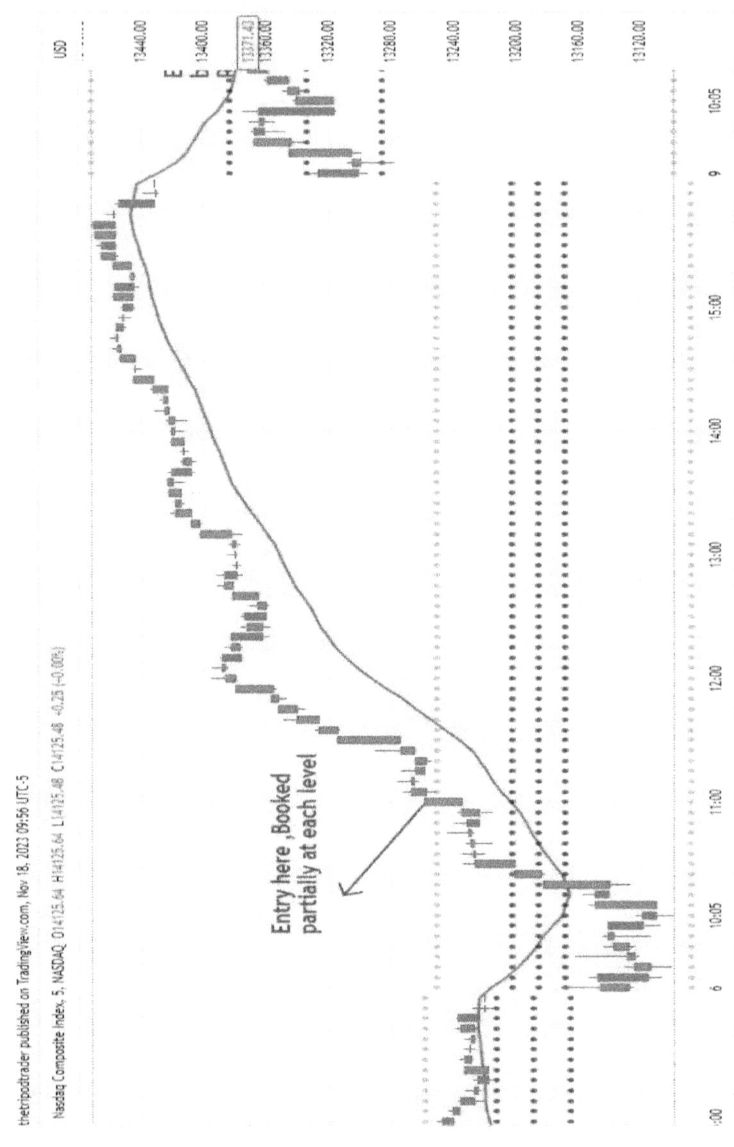
thetripodtrader published on TradingView.com, Nov 18, 2023 09:56 UTC-5
Nasdaq Composite Index, 5, NASDAQ O14125.64 H14125.64 L14125.48 C14125.48 -0.25 (-0.00%)
Entry here ,Booked partially at each level
USD
13440.00
13400.00
13371.43
13360.00
13320.00
13280.00
13240.00
13200.00
13160.00
13120.00
10:05
9
15:00
14:00
13:00
12:00
11:00
10:05
6
TradingView

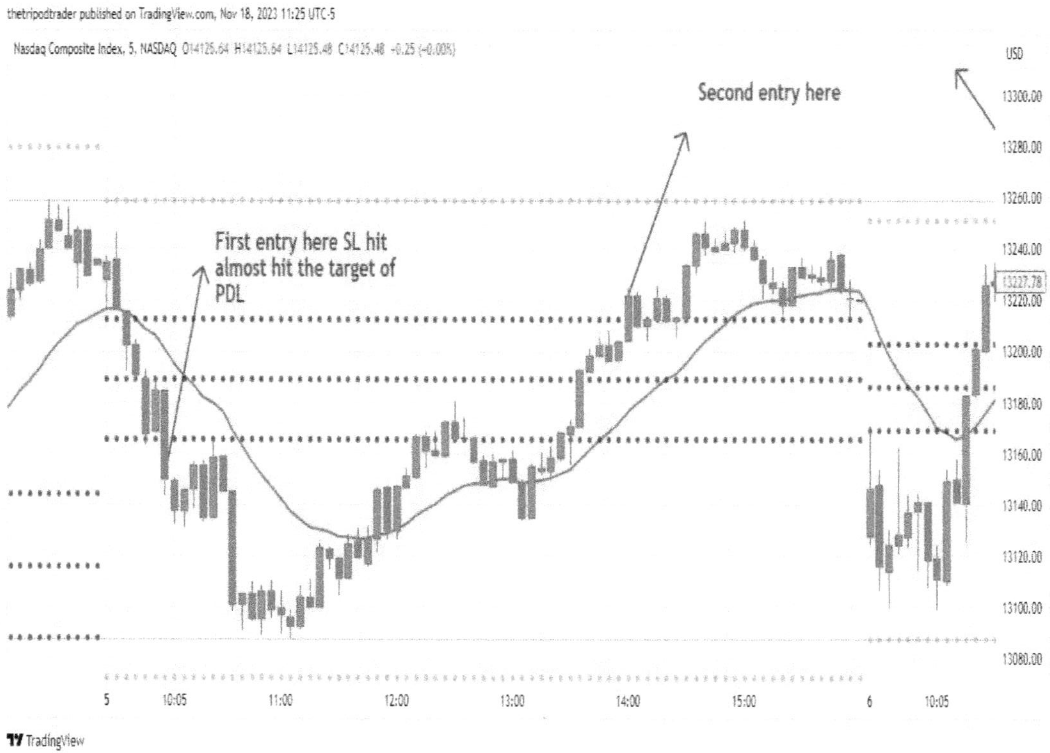
thetripodtrader published on TradingView.com, Nov 18, 2023 11:25 UTC-5
Nasdaq Composite Index, 5, NASDAQ O14125.64 H14125.64 L14125.48 C14125.48 −0.25 (−0.00%)
Second entry here
First entry here SL hit almost hit the target of PDL
USD
13300.00
13280.00
13260.00
13240.00
13227.78
13220.00
13200.00
13180.00
13160.00
13140.00
13120.00
13100.00
13080.00
5
10:05
11:00
12:00
13:00
14:00
15:00
6
10:05
TradingView

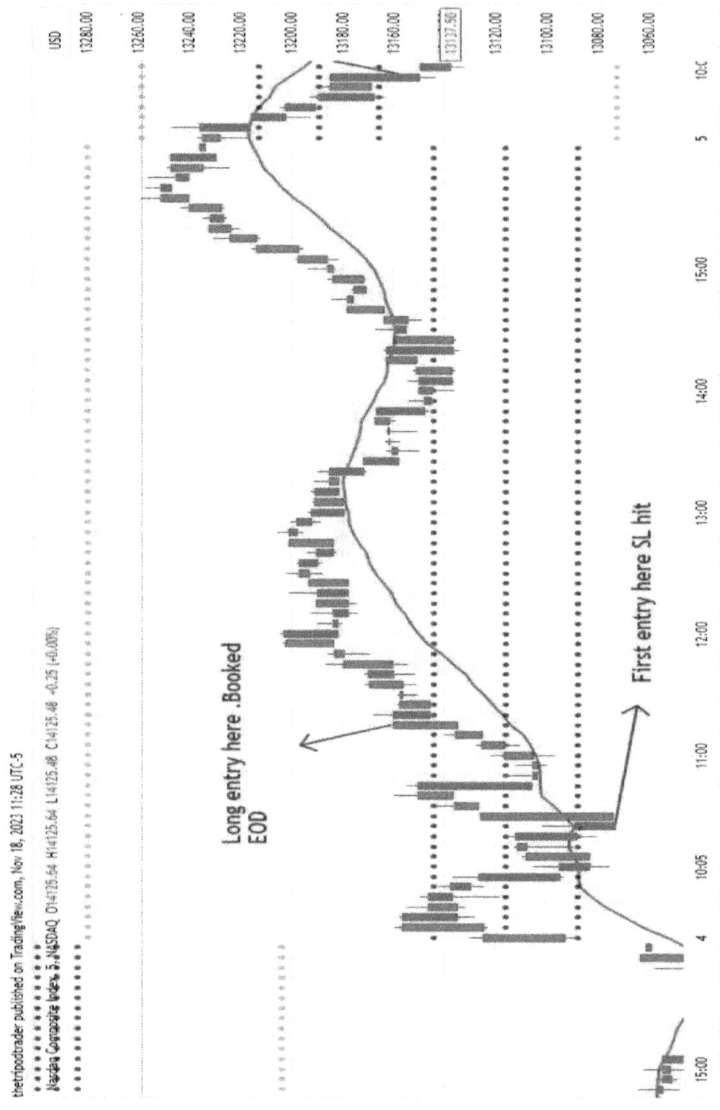
thetripodtrader published on TradingView.com, Nov 18, 2023 11:28 UTC-5
Nasdaq Composite Index, 5, NASDAQ O14125.64 H14125.64 L14125.48 C14125.48 -0.25 (-0.00%)
Long entry here .Booked EOD
First entry here SL hit
USD
13280.00
13260.00
13240.00
13220.00
13200.00
13180.00
13160.00
13137.50
13120.00
13100.00
13080.00
13060.00
15:00
4
10:05
11:00
12:00
13:00
14:00
15:00
5
TradingView

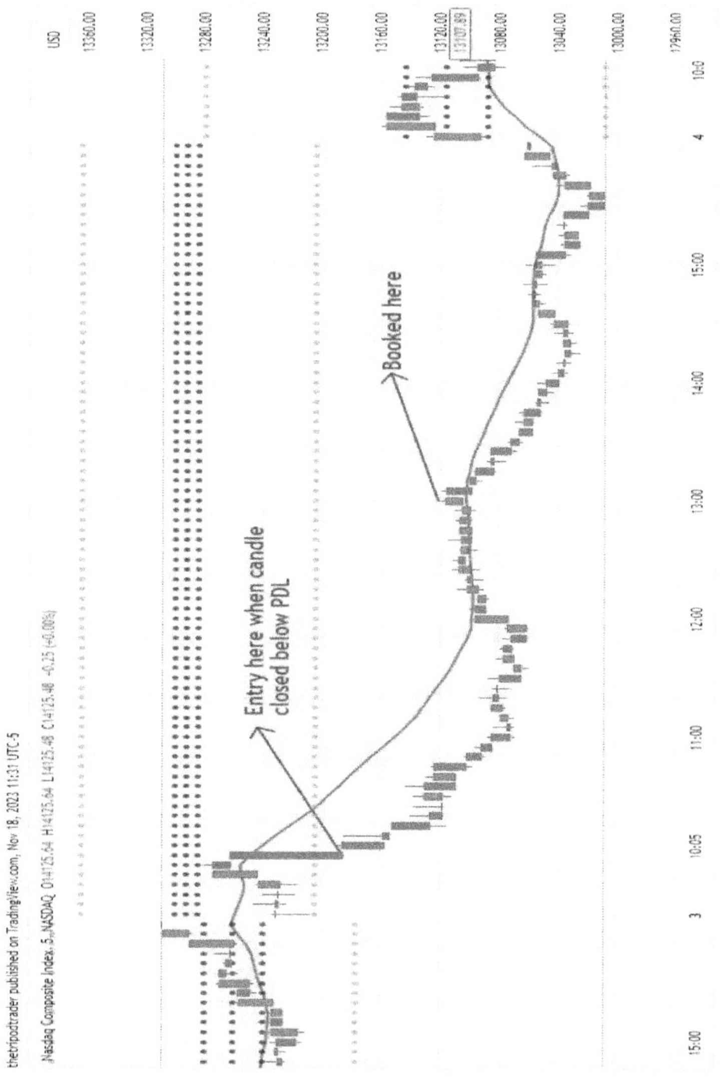
thetripodtrader published on TradingView.com, Nov 18, 2023 11:31 UTC-5
Entry here when candle closed below PDL
Booked here
USD
13360.00
13320.00
13280.00
13240.00
13200.00
13160.00
13120.00
13080.00
13040.00
13000.00
15:00
3
10:05
11:00
12:00
13:00
14:00
15:00
4
TradingView

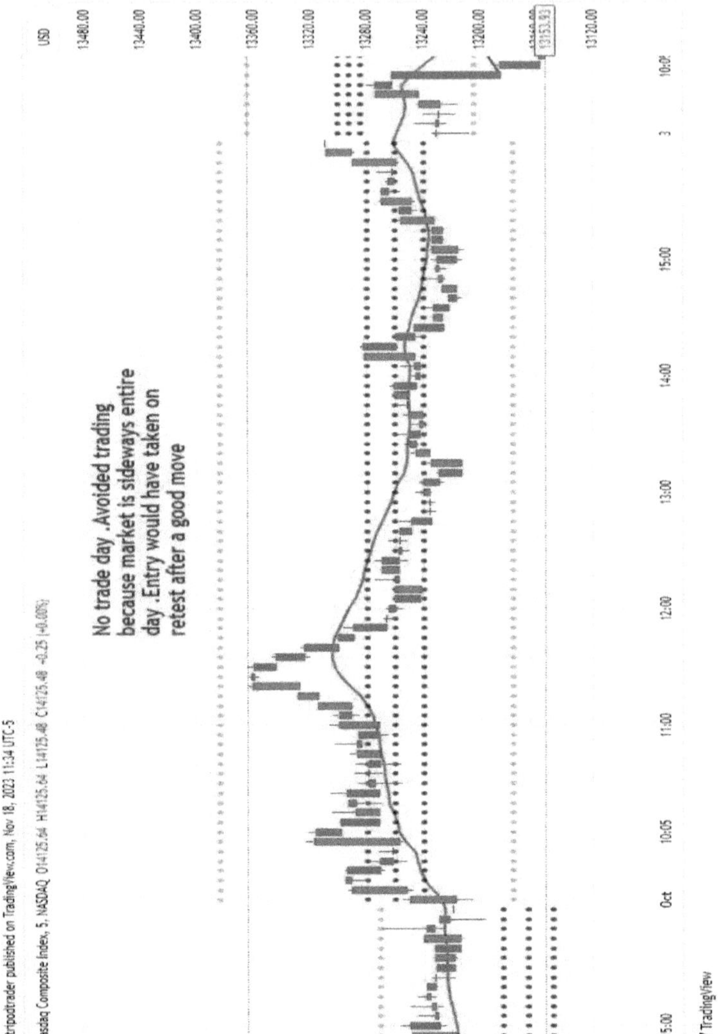
thetripodtrader published on TradingView.com, Nov 18, 2023 11:34 UTC-5
No trade day .Avoided trading because market is sideways entire day .Entry would have taken on retest after a good move
TradingView

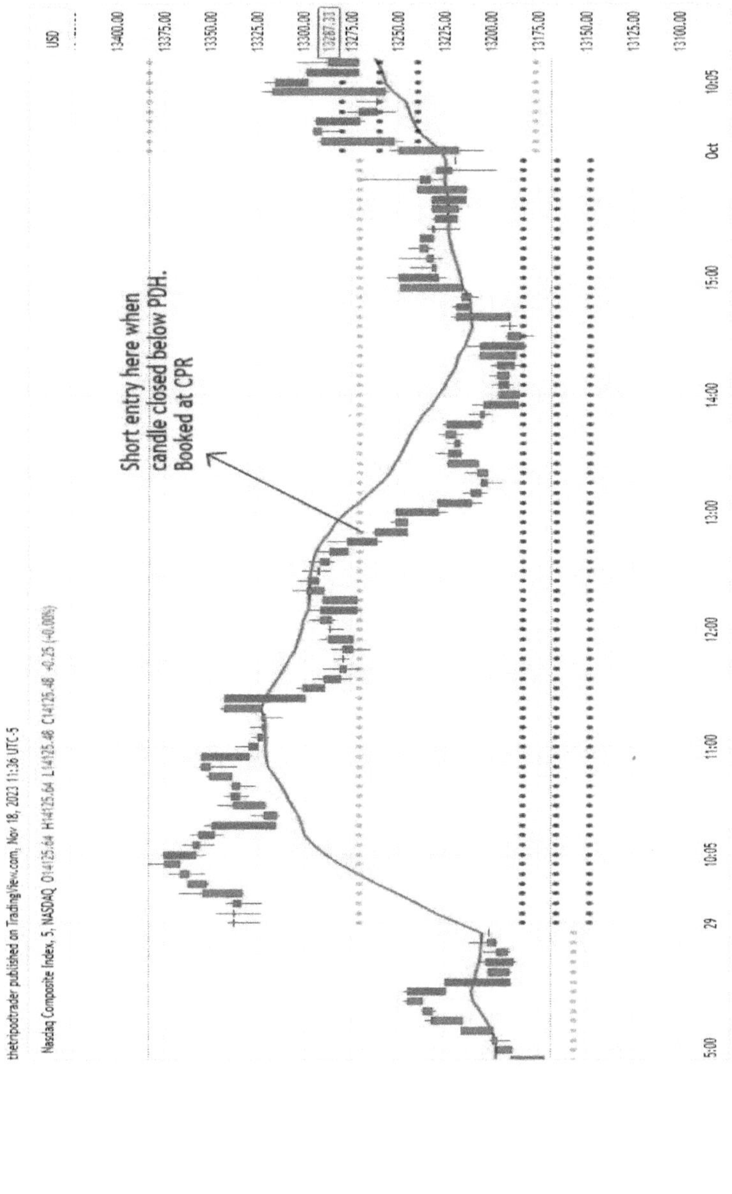
thetripodtrader published on TradingView.com, Nov 18, 2023 11:36 UTC-5
Nasdaq Composite Index, 5, NASDAQ O14125.64 H14125.64 L14125.48 C14125.48 +0.25 (+0.00%)
Short entry here when candle closed below PDH. Booked at CPR
TradingView

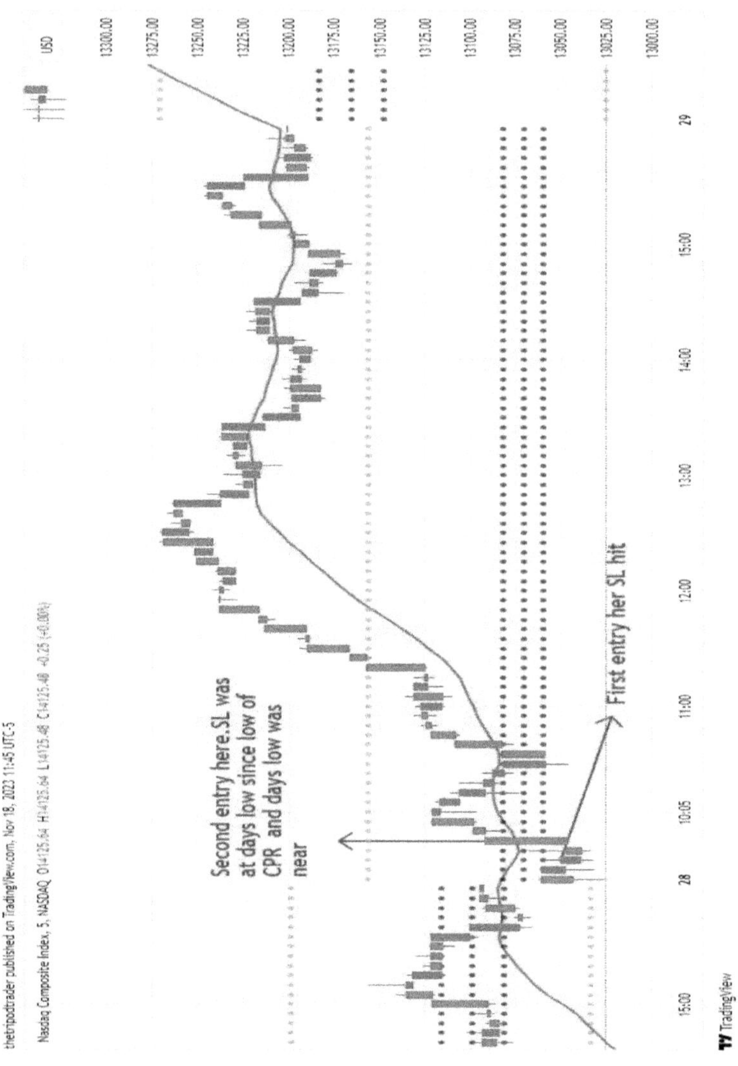
thetripodtrader published on TradingView.com, Nov 18, 2023 11:45 UTC-5
Second entry here.SL was at days low since low of CPR and days low was near
First entry her SL hit
TradingView

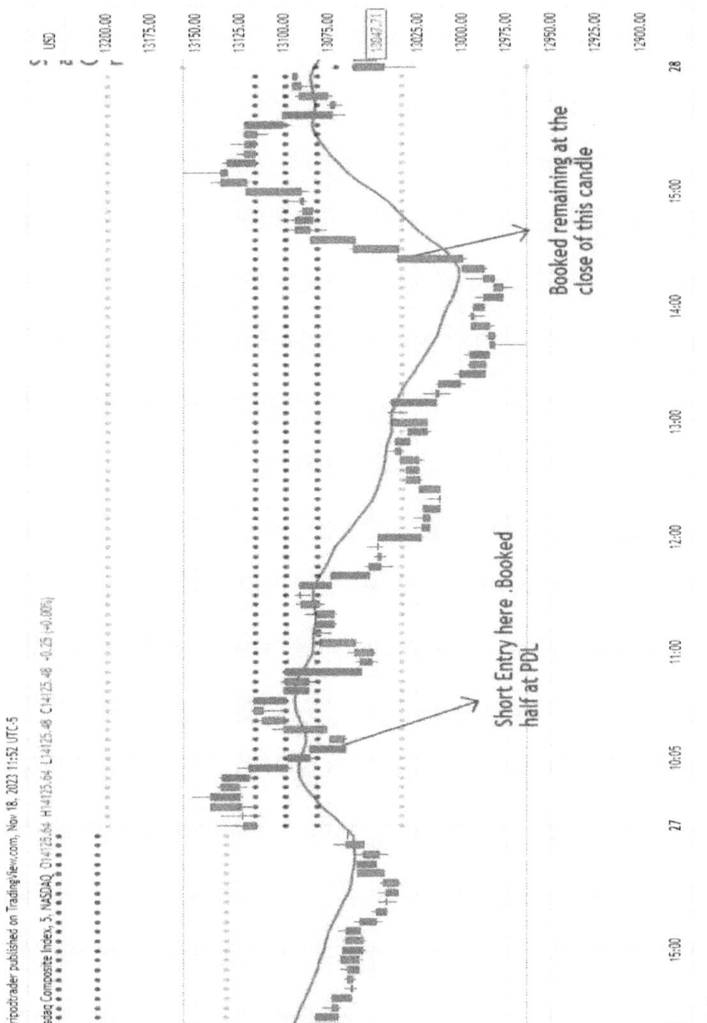
thetripodtrader published on TradingView.com, Nov 18, 2023 11:52 UTC-5
Short Entry here .Booked half at PDL
Booked remaining at the close of this candle
13200.00
13175.00
13150.00
13125.00
13100.00
13075.00
13025.00
13000.00
12975.00
12950.00
12925.00
12900.00
4:15
15:00
27
10:05
11:00
12:00
13:00
14:00
15:00
28
TradingView

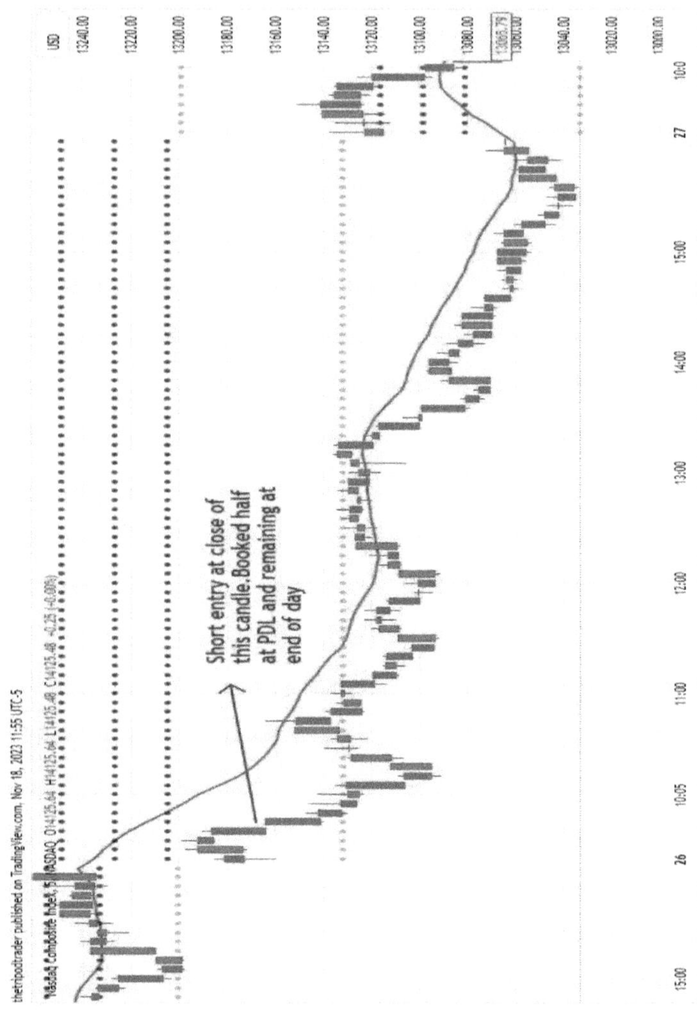
thetripodtrader published on TradingView.com, Nov 18, 2023 11:55 UTC-5
Short entry at close of this candle.Booked half at PDL and remaining at end of day
TradingView

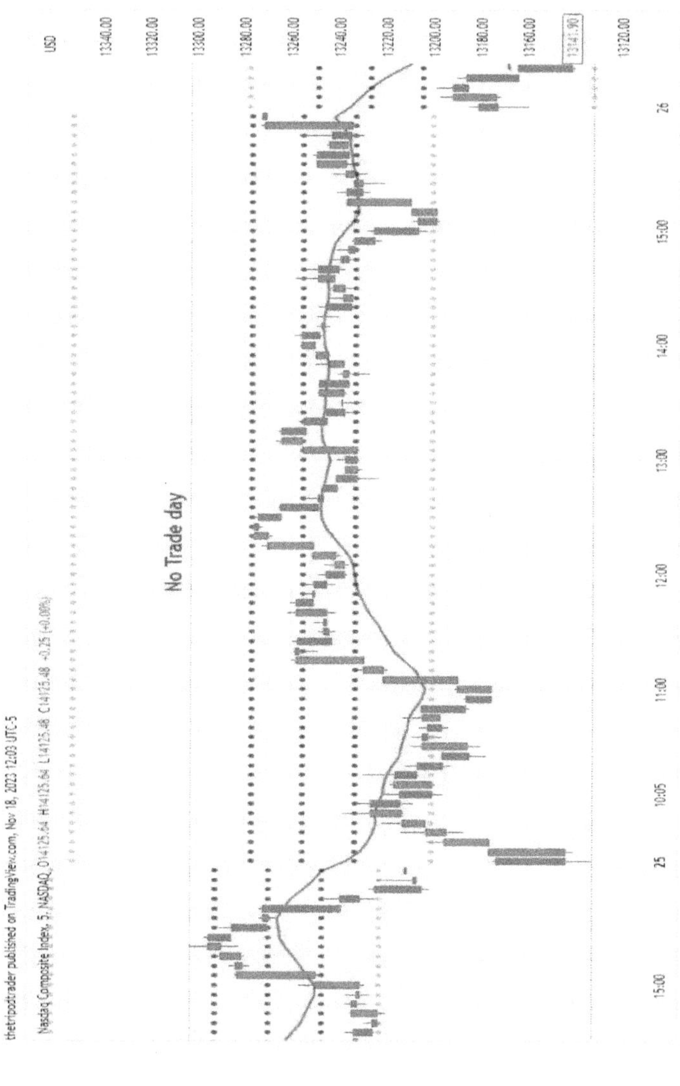
thetripodtrader published on TradingView.com, Nov 18, 2023 12:03 UTC-5
No Trade day
TradingView

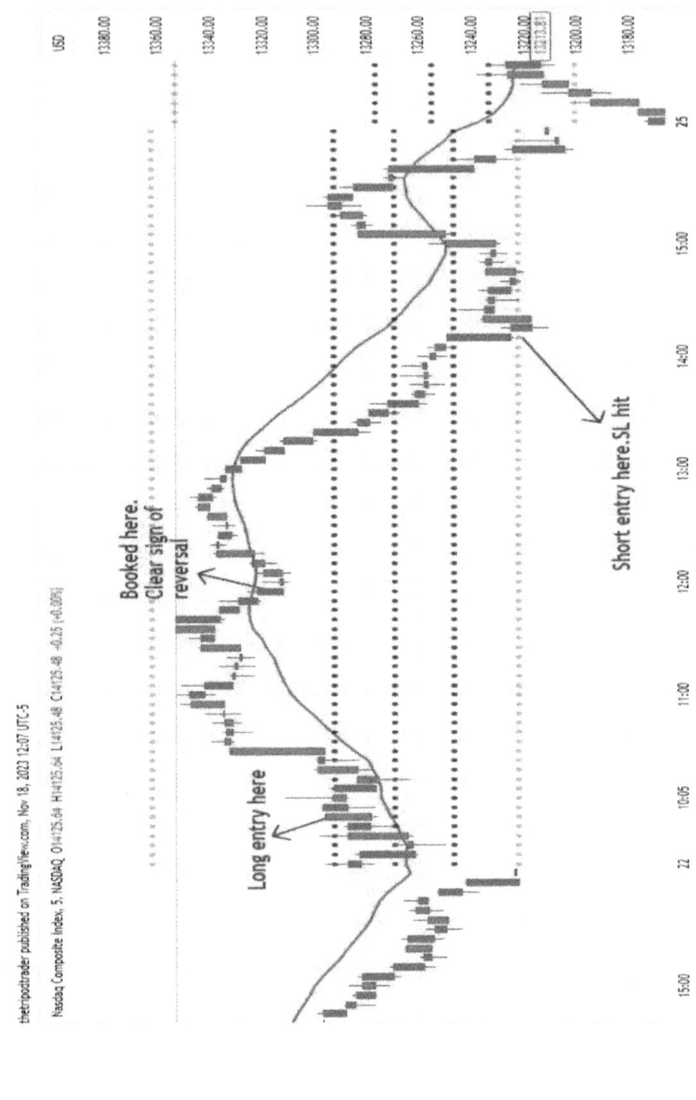
thetripodtrader published on TradingView.com, Nov 18, 2023 12:07 UTC-5
Booked here. Clear sign of reversal
Long entry here
Short entry here.SL hit
TradingView

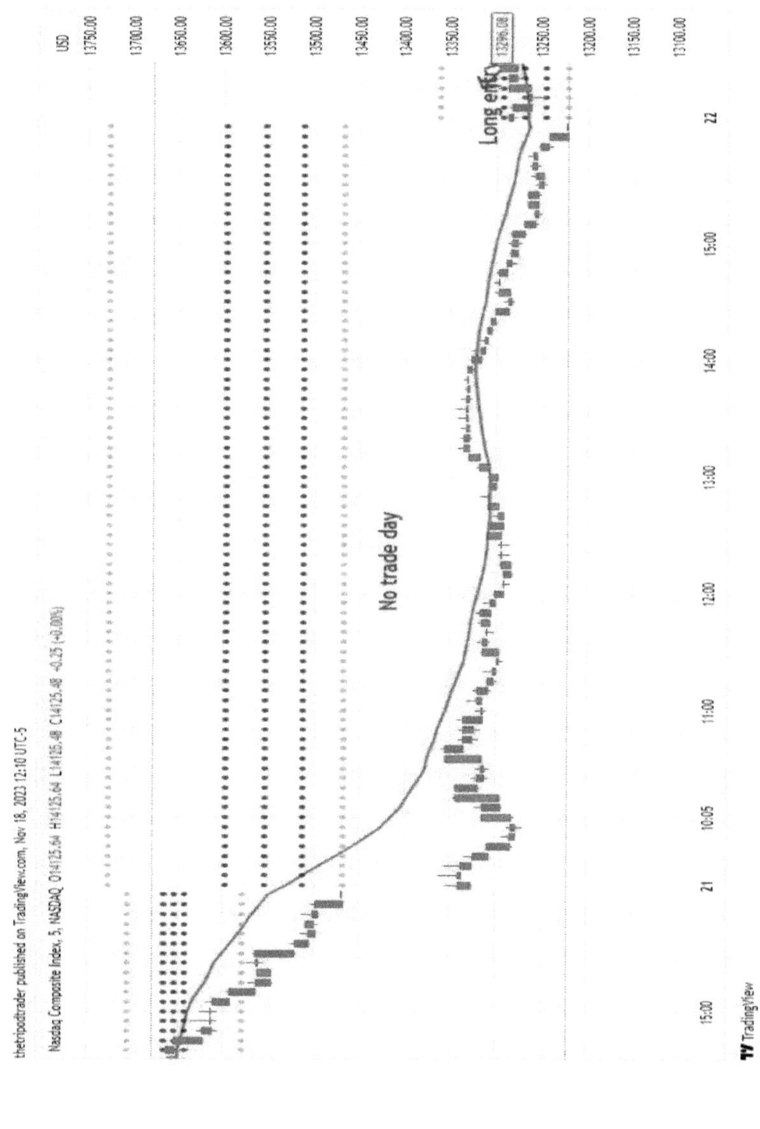
thetripodtrader published on TradingView.com, Nov 18, 2023 12:10 UTC-5
No trade day
TradingView

thetripodtrader published on TradingView.com, Nov 18, 2023 12:12 UTC-5
Nasdaq Composite Index, 5, NASDAQ O14125.64 H14125.64 L14125.48 C14125.48 -0.25 (+0.00%)
USD
13800.00
13760.00
13720.00
13680.00
13640.00
13600.00
13560.00
13520.00
13480.00
13440.00
Short entry here .Market broke out of day range and candle closed below PDL
20
10:05
11:00
12:00
13:00
14:00
15:00
21
10:05
TradingView

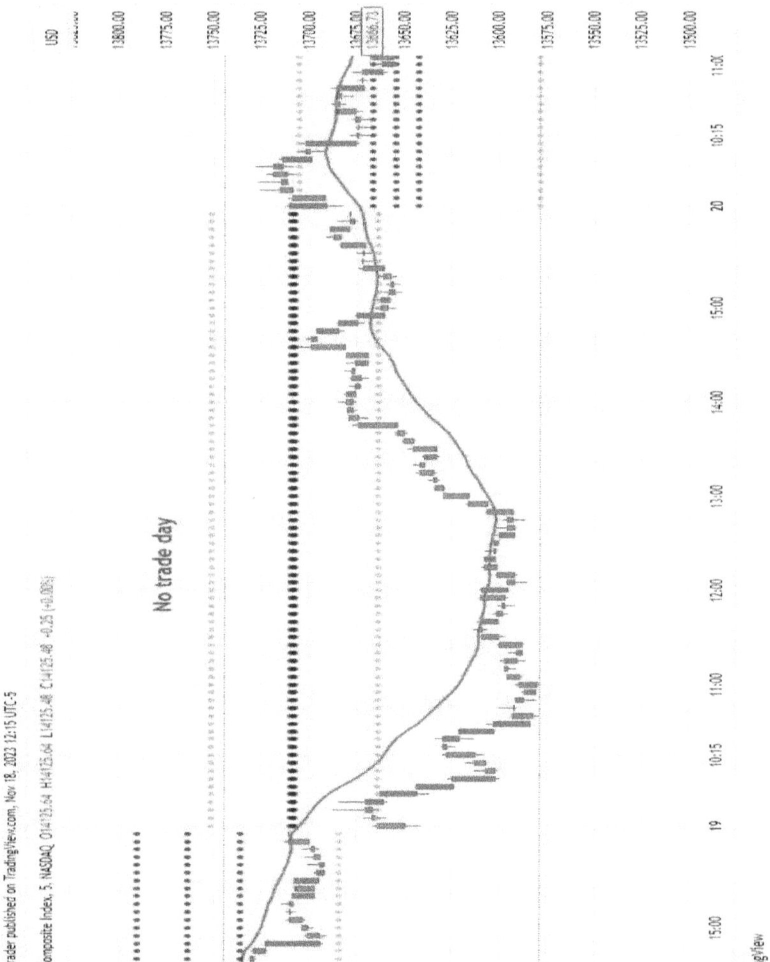
thetripodtrader published on TradingView.com, Nov 18, 2023 12:15 UTC-5
No trade day
TradingView

thetripodtrader published on TradingView.com, Nov 18, 2023 12:17 UTC-5
Nasdaq Composite Index, 5, NASDAQ O14125.64 H14125.64 L14125.48 C14125.48 −0.25 (−0.00%)
USD
No trade day
13840.00
13820.00
13800.00
13780.00
13760.00
13740.00
13720.00
13700.00
13680.00
13660.00
13640.00
14:00
15:00
18
10:15
11:00
12:00
13:00
14:00
15:00
19
10:15
TradingView

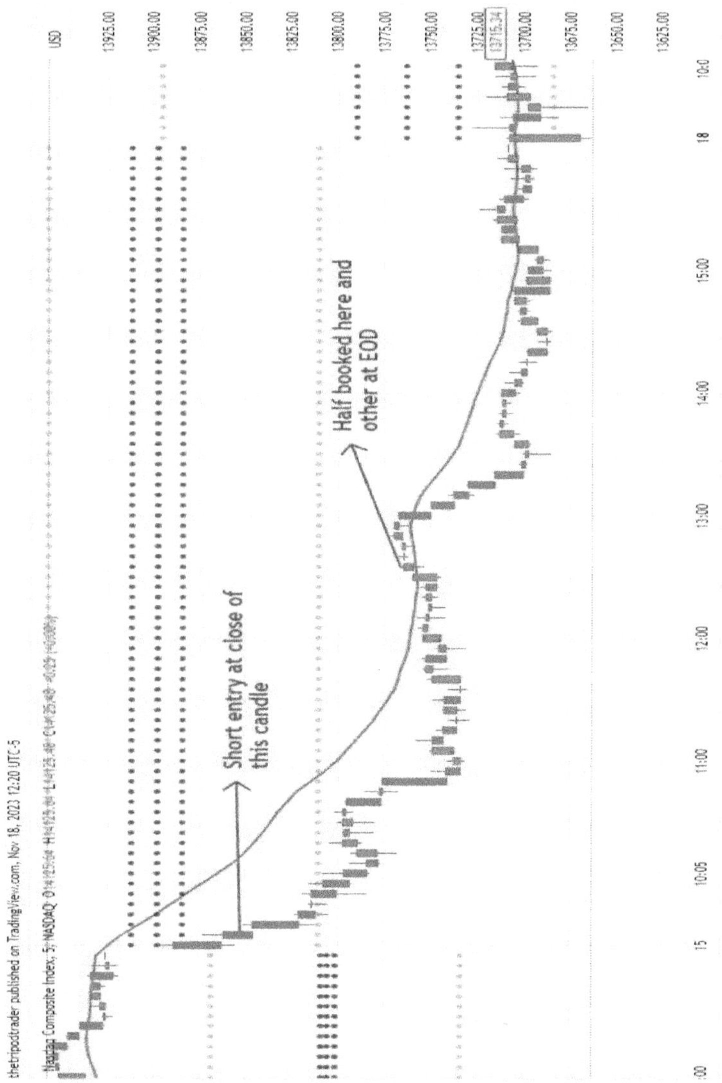

shetripodtrader published on TradingView.com, Nov 18, 2023 12:20 UTC-5
Nasdaq Composite Index, 5, NASDAQ
Short entry at close of this candle
Half booked here and other at EOD
USD
13925.00
13900.00
13875.00
13850.00
13825.00
13800.00
13775.00
13750.00
13725.00
13715.34
13700.00
13675.00
13650.00
13625.00
15
10:05
11:00
12:00
13:00
14:00
15:00
18
TradingView

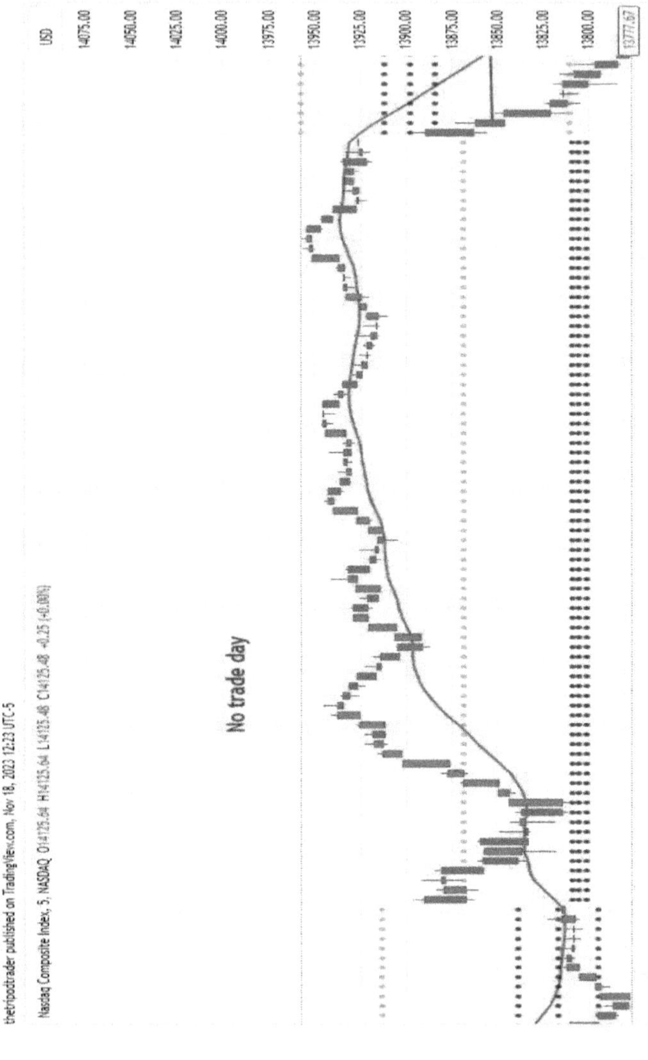
thetripodtrader published on TradingView.com, Nov 18, 2023 12:23 UTC-5
No trade day
USD
14075.00
14050.00
14025.00
14000.00
13975.00
13950.00
13925.00
13900.00
13875.00
13850.00
13825.00
13800.00
13777.67
TradingView

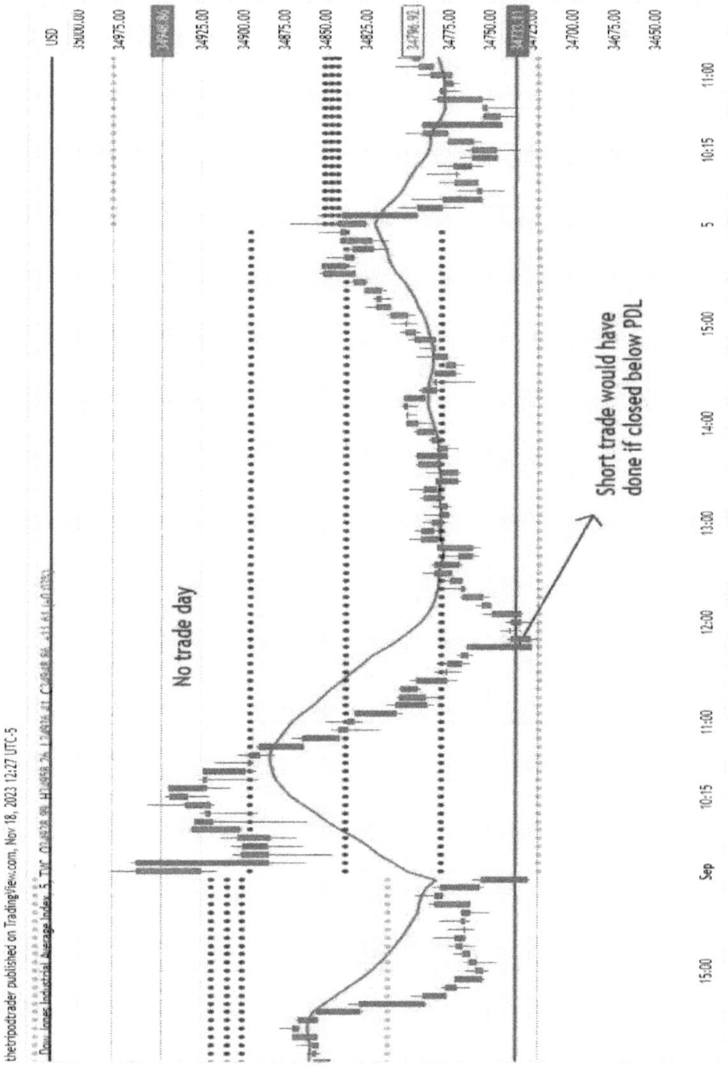
thetripodtrader published on TradingView.com, Nov 18, 2023 12:27 UTC-5
Dow Jones Industrial Average Index, 5, TVC
No trade day
Short trade would have
done if closed below PDL
TradingView

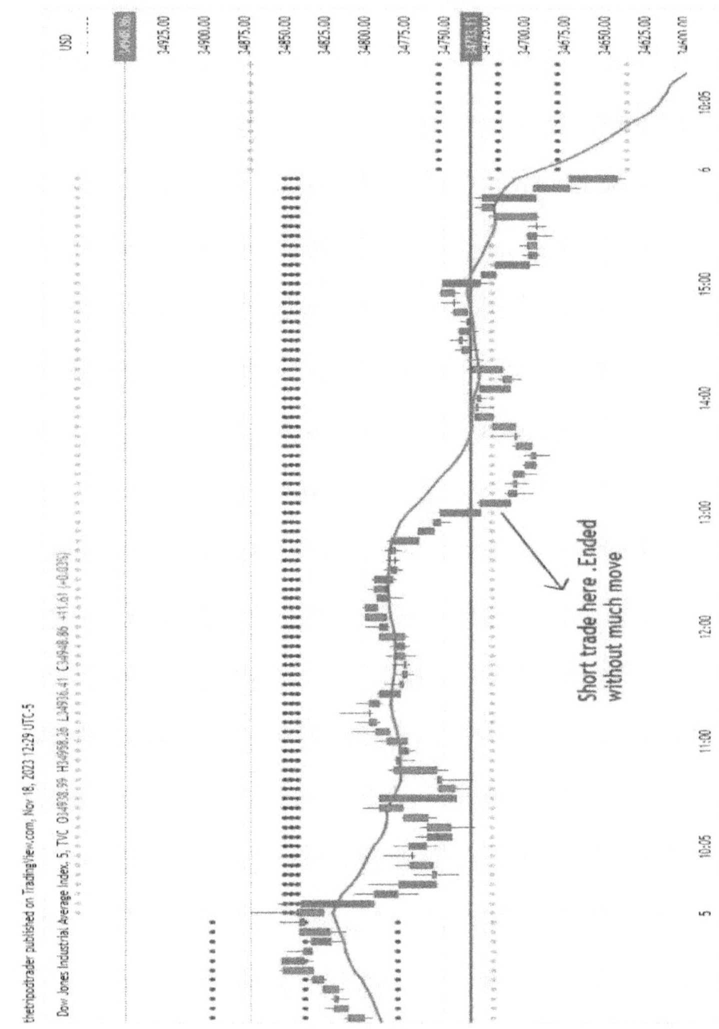
thetripodtrader published on TradingView.com, Nov 18, 2023 12:29 UTC-5
Dow Jones Industrial Average Index, 5, TVC O34938.99 H34958.36 L34936.41 C34948.86 +11.61 (+0.03%)
USD
34925.00
34900.00
34875.00
34850.00
34825.00
34800.00
34775.00
34750.00
34733.11
34725.00
34700.00
34675.00
34650.00
34625.00
34600.00
5
10:05
11:00
12:00
13:00
14:00
15:00
6
10:05
Short trade here .Ended
without much move
TradingView

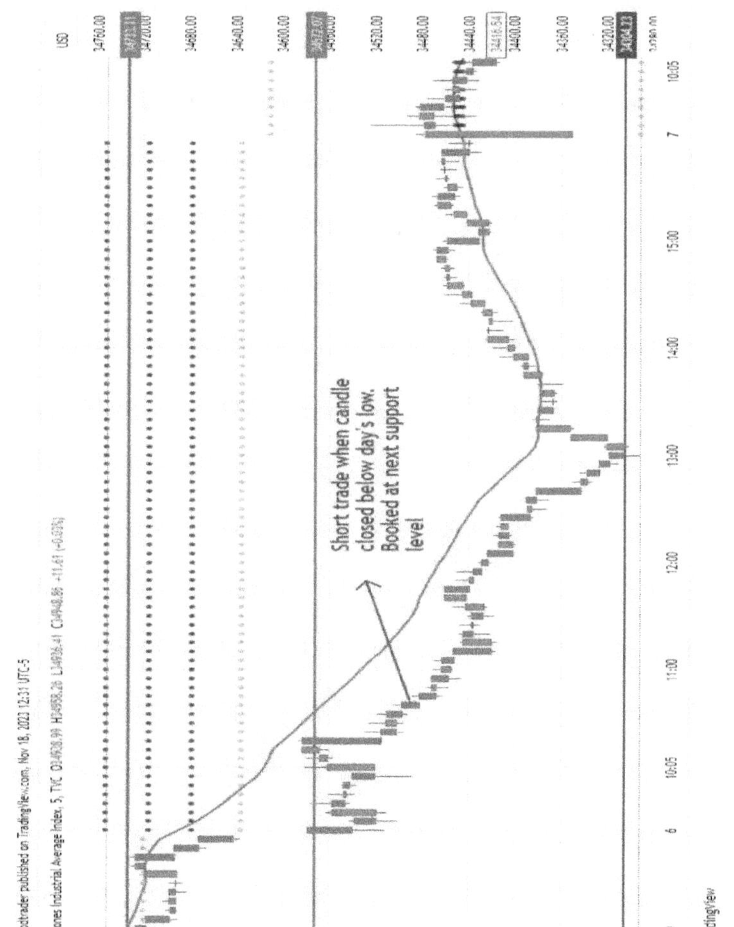
thetripodtrader published on TradingView.com, Nov 18, 2022 12:31 UTC-5
Short trade when candle closed below day's low. Booked at next support level
TradingView

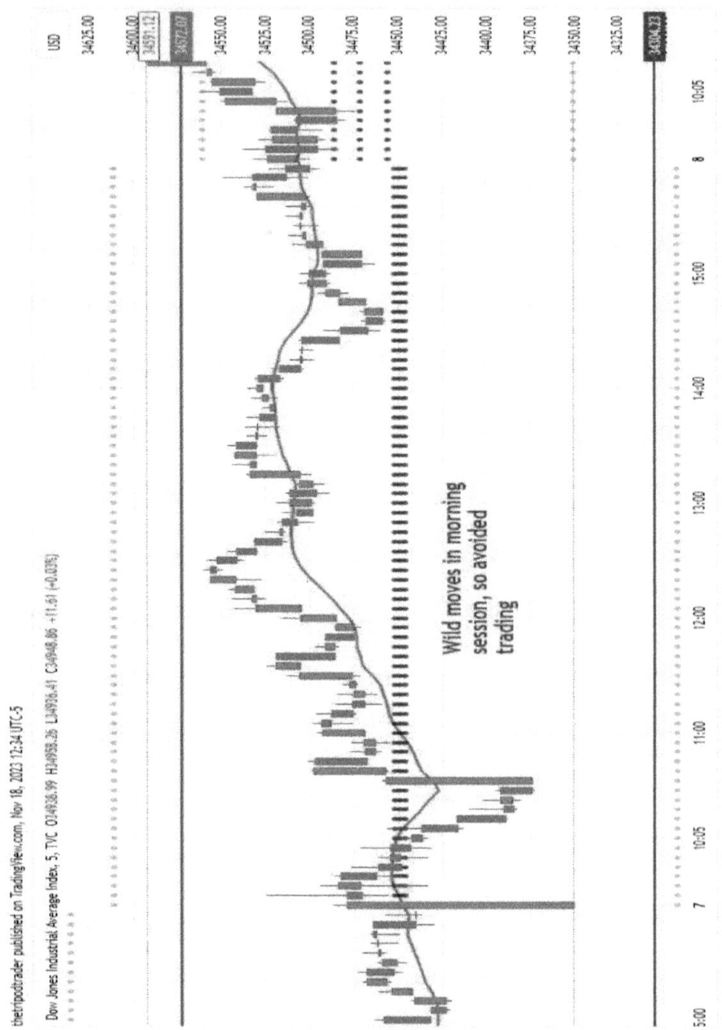
thetripodtrader published on TradingView.com, Nov 18, 2023 12:34 UTC-5
Dow Jones Industrial Average Index, 5, TVC
Wild moves in morning session, so avoided trading
USD
34625.00
34600.00
34591.12
34572.07
34550.00
34525.00
34500.00
34475.00
34450.00
34425.00
34400.00
34375.00
34350.00
34325.00
34304.23
5:00
7
10:05
11:00
12:00
13:00
14:00
15:00
8
10:05
TradingView

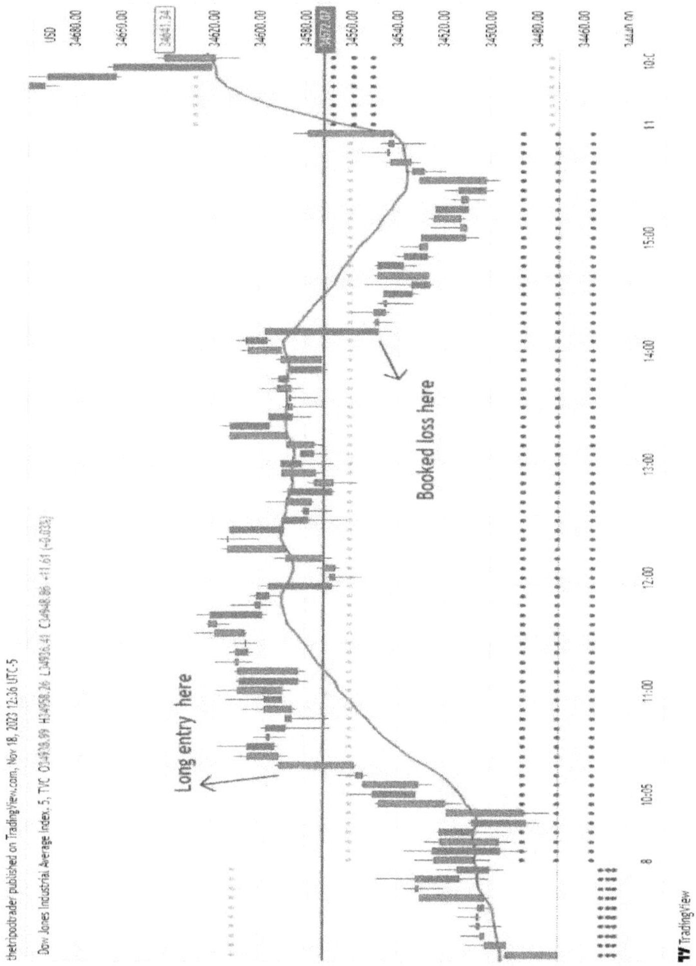
thetripodtrader published on TradingView.com, Nov 18, 2023 12:36 UTC-5
Long entry here
Booked loss here
TradingView

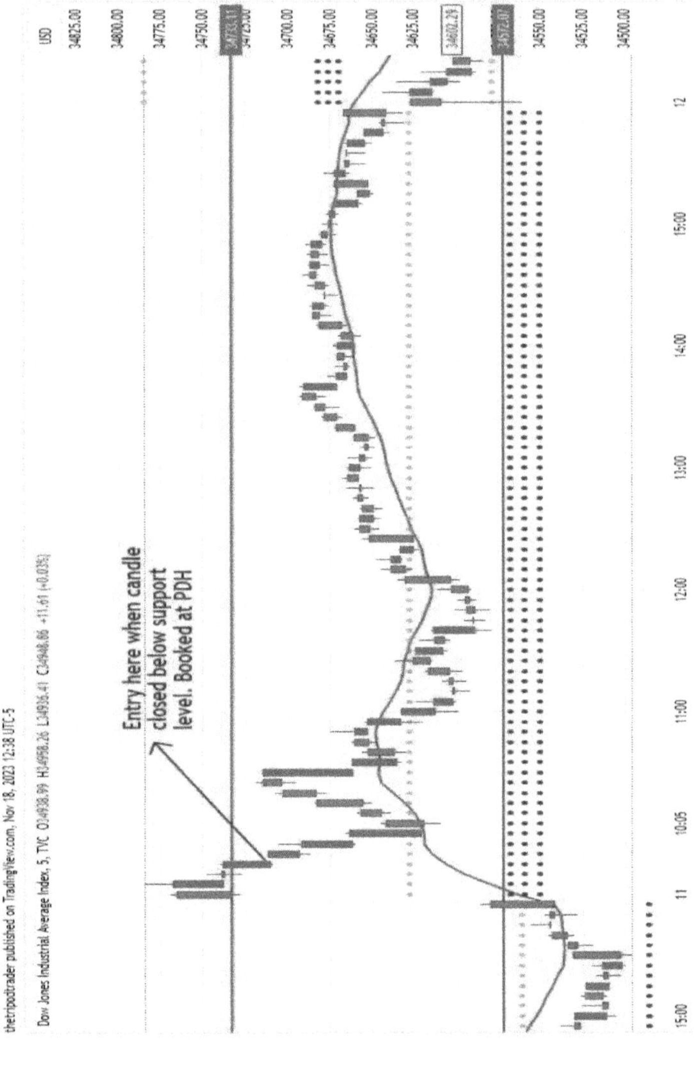
thetripodtrader published on TradingView.com, Nov 18, 2023 12:38 UTC-5
Dow Jones Industrial Average Index, 5, TVC
Entry here when candle closed below support level. Booked at PDH
TradingView

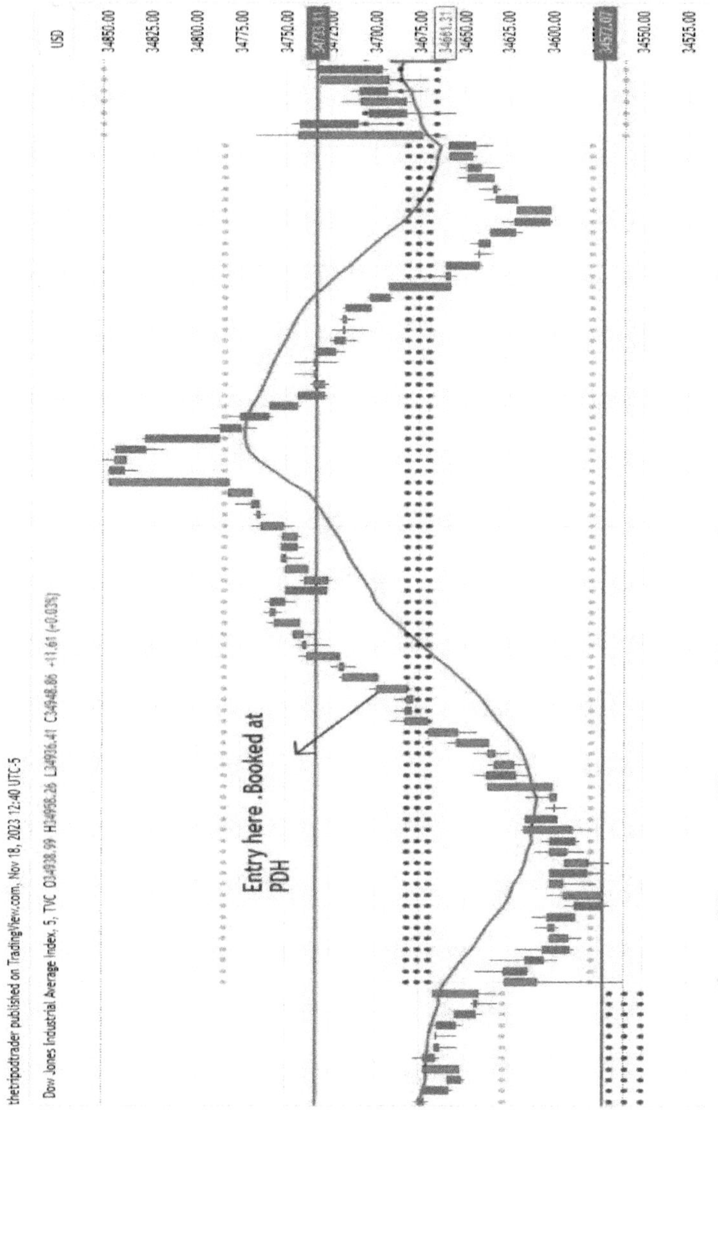
thetripodtrader published on TradingView.com, Nov 18, 2023 12:40 UTC-5
Dow Jones Industrial Average Index, 5, TVC O34938.99 H34958.26 L34936.41 C34948.86 +11.61 (+0.03%)
Entry here .Booked at PDH
USD
34850.00
34825.00
34800.00
34775.00
34750.00
34725.00
34700.00
34675.00
34650.00
34625.00
34600.00
34550.00
34525.00
12
10:05
11:00
12:00
13:00
14:00
15:00
13
10
TradingView

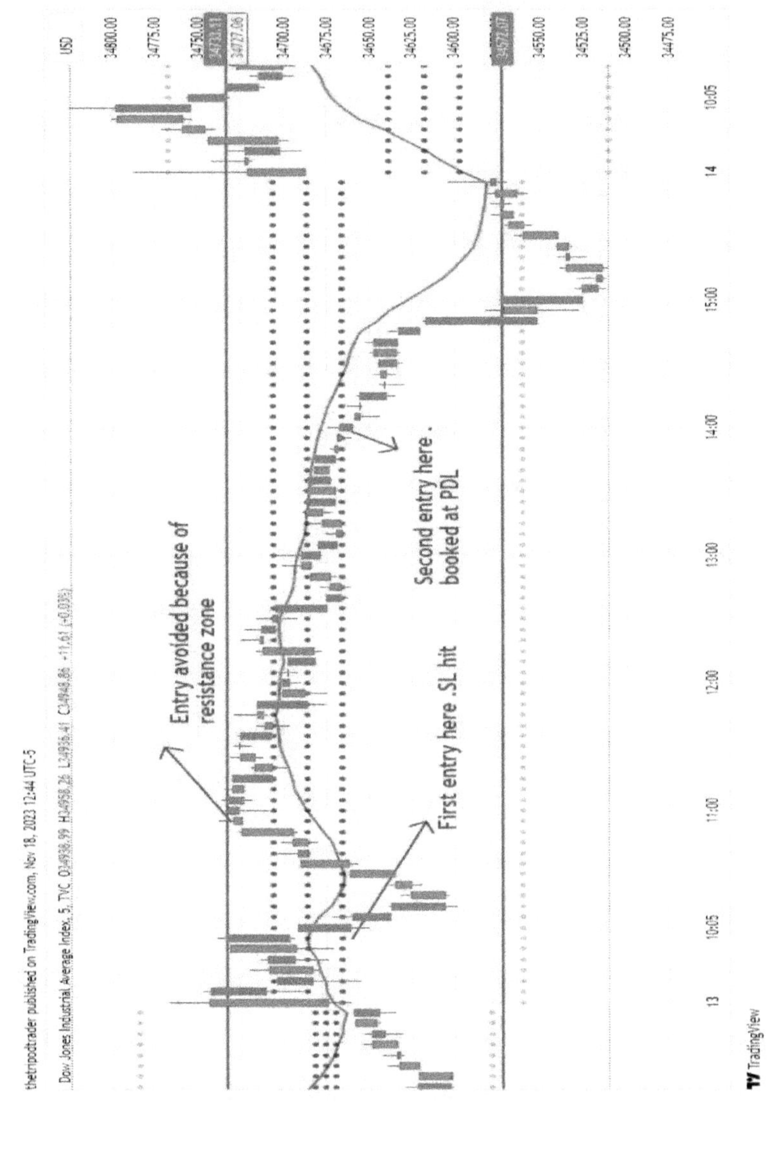
thetripodtrader published on TradingView.com, Nov 18, 2023 12:44 UTC-5
Entry avoided because of resistance zone
First entry here .SL hit
Second entry here .
booked at PDL
USD
34800.00
34775.00
34750.00
34727.06
34700.00
34675.00
34650.00
34625.00
34600.00
34550.00
34525.00
34500.00
34475.00
13
10:05
11:00
12:00
13:00
14:00
15:00
14
10:05
TradingView

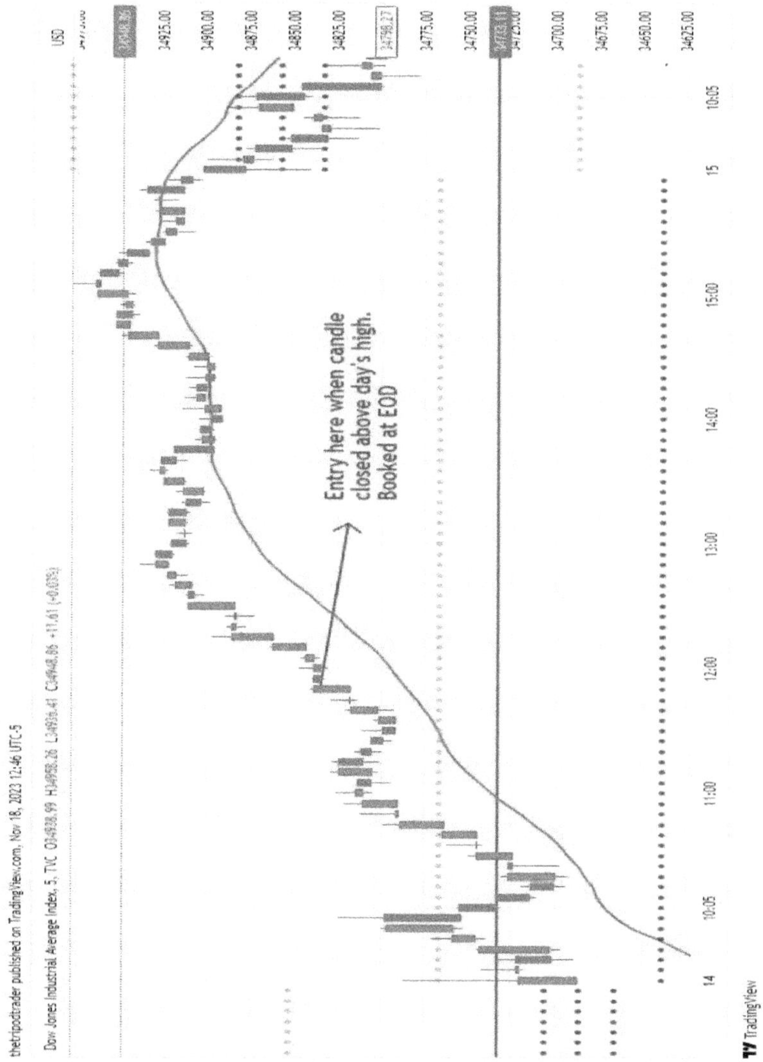
thetripodtrader published on TradingView.com, Nov 18, 2023 12:46 UTC-5
Dow Jones Industrial Average Index, 5, TVC
Entry here when candle closed above day's high. Booked at EOD
TradingView

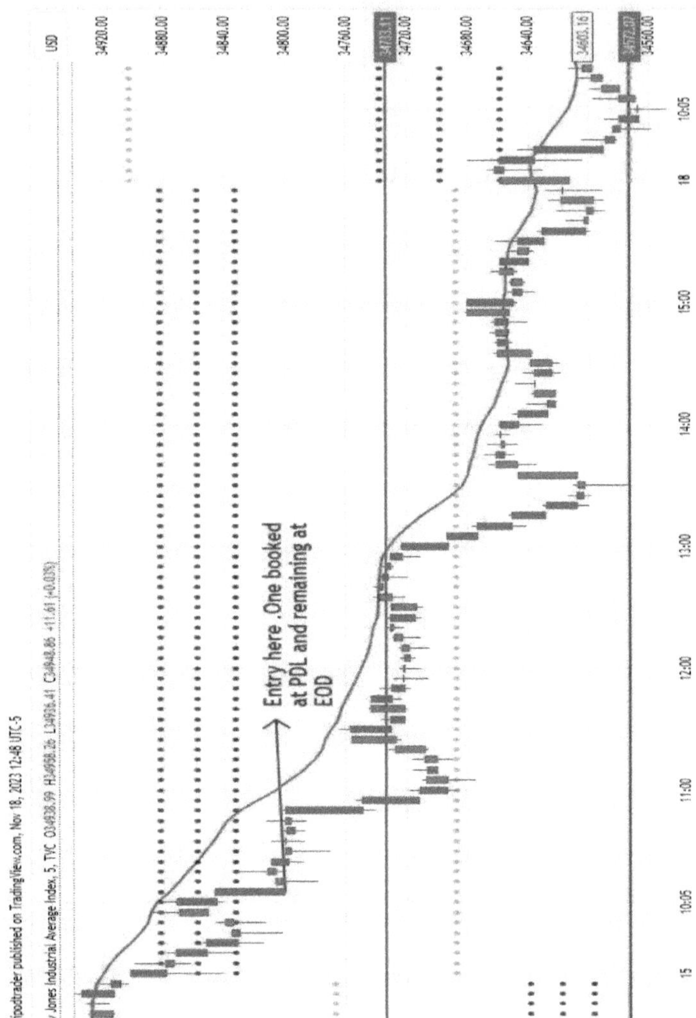
thetripodtrader published on TradingView.com, Nov 18, 2023 12:48 UTC-5
Dow Jones Industrial Average Index, 5, TVC
Entry here .One booked at PDL and remaining at EOD
USD
34920.00
34880.00
34840.00
34800.00
34760.00
34720.00
34680.00
34640.00
34600.00
34603.16
15
10:05
11:00
12:00
13:00
14:00
15:00
18
10:05
TradingView

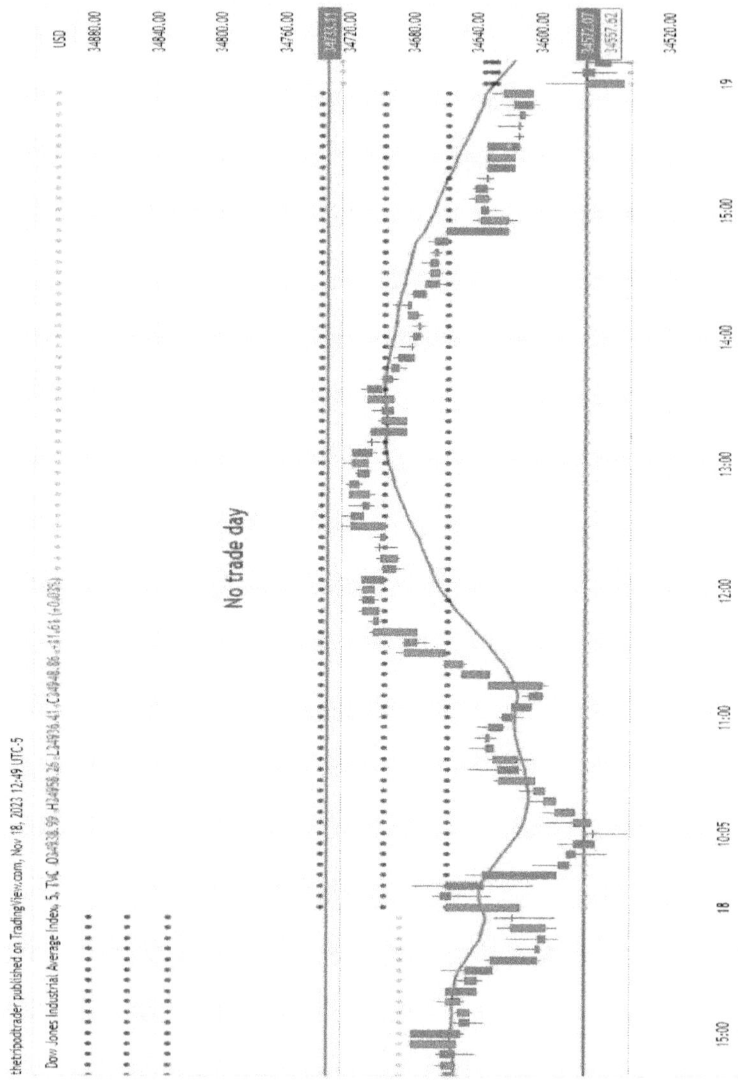
thetripodtrader published on TradingView.com, Nov 18, 2023 12:49 UTC-5
No trade day
USD
34880.00
34840.00
34800.00
34760.00
34720.00
34680.00
34640.00
34600.00
34520.00
15:00
18
10:05
11:00
12:00
13:00
14:00
15:00
19
TradingView

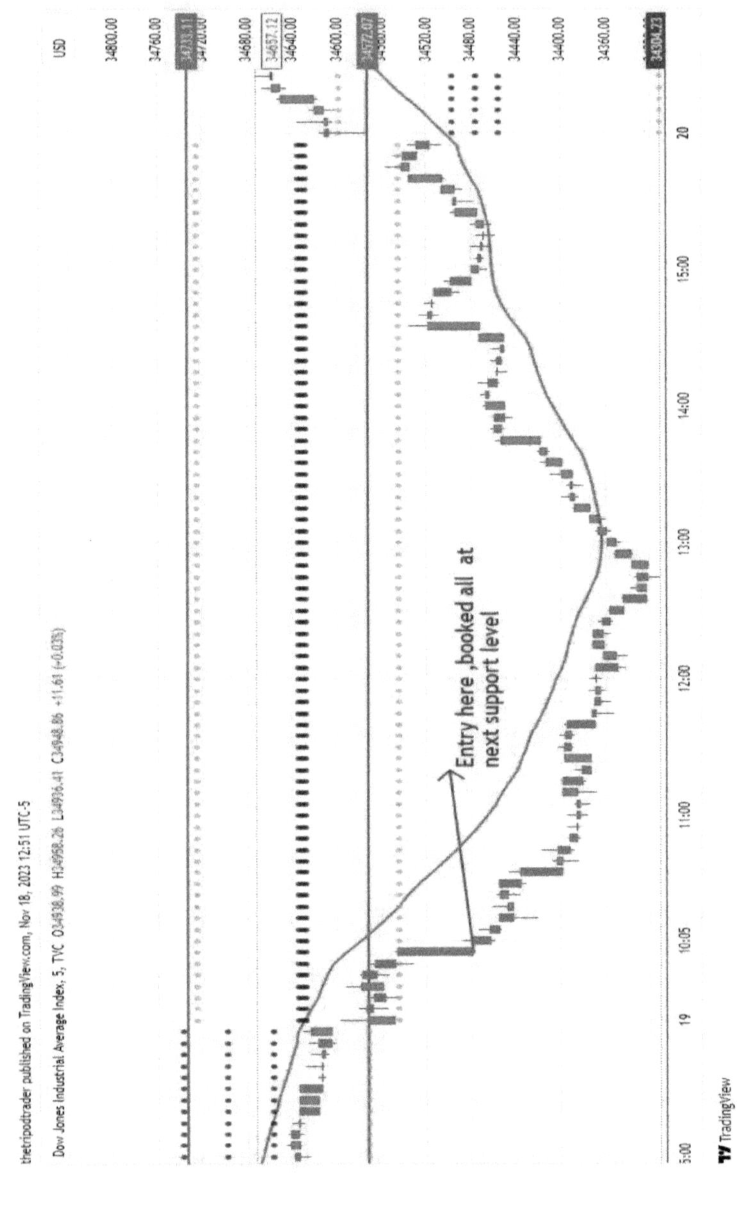
thetripodtrader published on TradingView.com, Nov 18, 2023 12:51 UTC-5
Dow Jones Industrial Average Index, 5, TVC O34938.99 H34958.26 L34936.41 C34948.86 +11.61 (+0.03%)
Entry here ,booked all at
next support level
TradingView

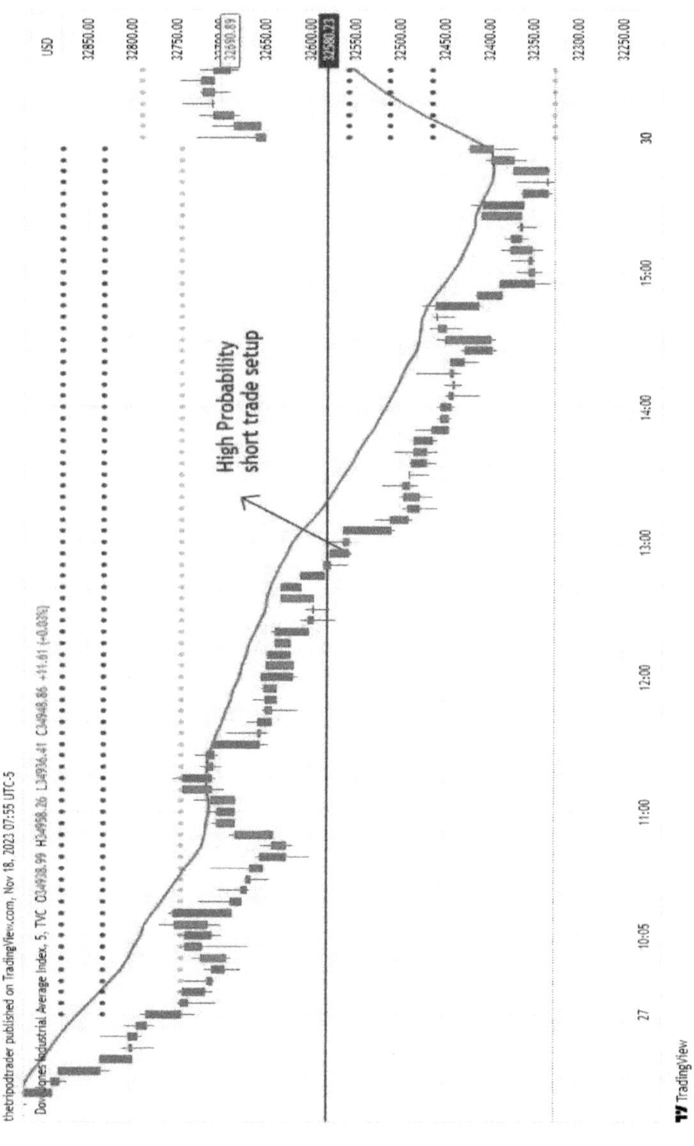

thetripodtrader published on TradingView.com, Nov 18, 2023 07:55 UTC-5
High Probability short trade setup
USD
32850.00
32800.00
32750.00
32650.00
32600.00
32550.00
32500.00
32450.00
32400.00
32350.00
32300.00
32250.00
27
10:05
11:00
12:00
13:00
14:00
15:00
30
TradingView

thetripodtrader published on TradingView.com, Nov 18, 2023 07:52 UTC-5
Dow Jones Industrial Average Index, 5, TVC
CPR by KGS 34928.66 34920.24 34937.07
EMA 20/50/100/200 34945.65
High Probability Short Trade Setup
USD
34275.00
34250.00
34225.00
34200.00
34175.00
34150.00
34125.00
34100.00
34087.98
34075.00
34050.00
34034.79
34025.00
34000.00
33975.00
33950.00
8
10:00
10:30
11:00
11:30
12:00
12:30
13:00
13:30
14:00
14:30
15:00
15:30
9
TradingView

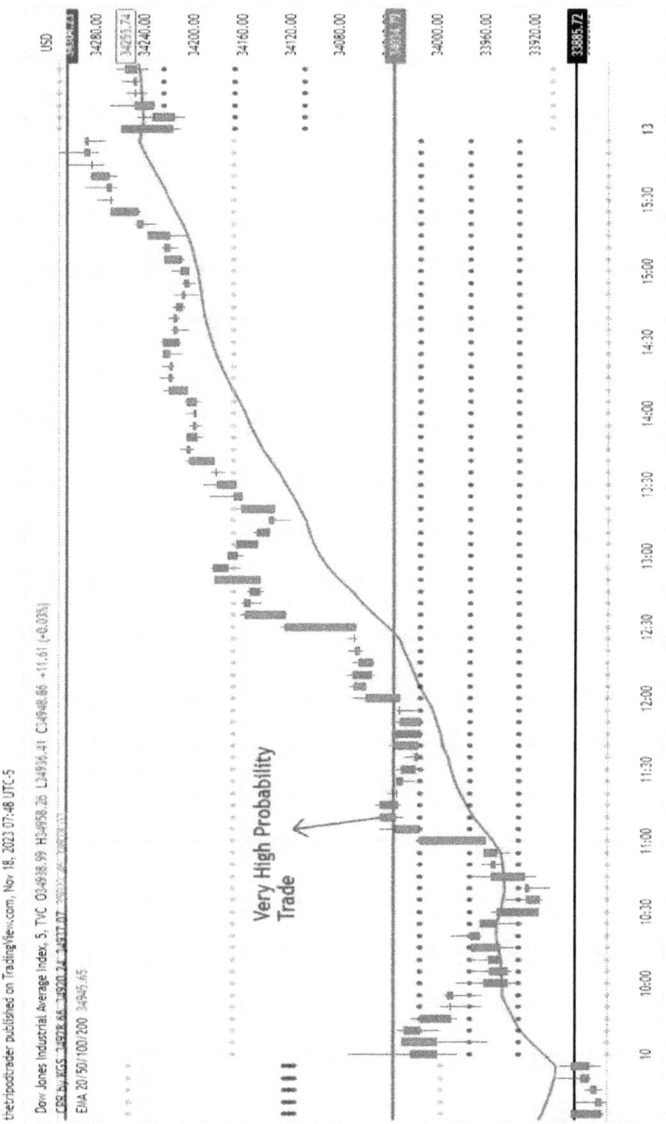
thetripodtrader published on TradingView.com, Nov 18, 2023 07:48 UTC-5
Very High Probability Trade
USD
34280.00
34240.00
34200.00
34160.00
34120.00
34080.00
34000.00
33960.00
33920.00
33885.72
10
10:00
10:30
11:00
11:30
12:00
12:30
13:00
13:30
14:00
14:30
15:00
15:30
13
TradingView

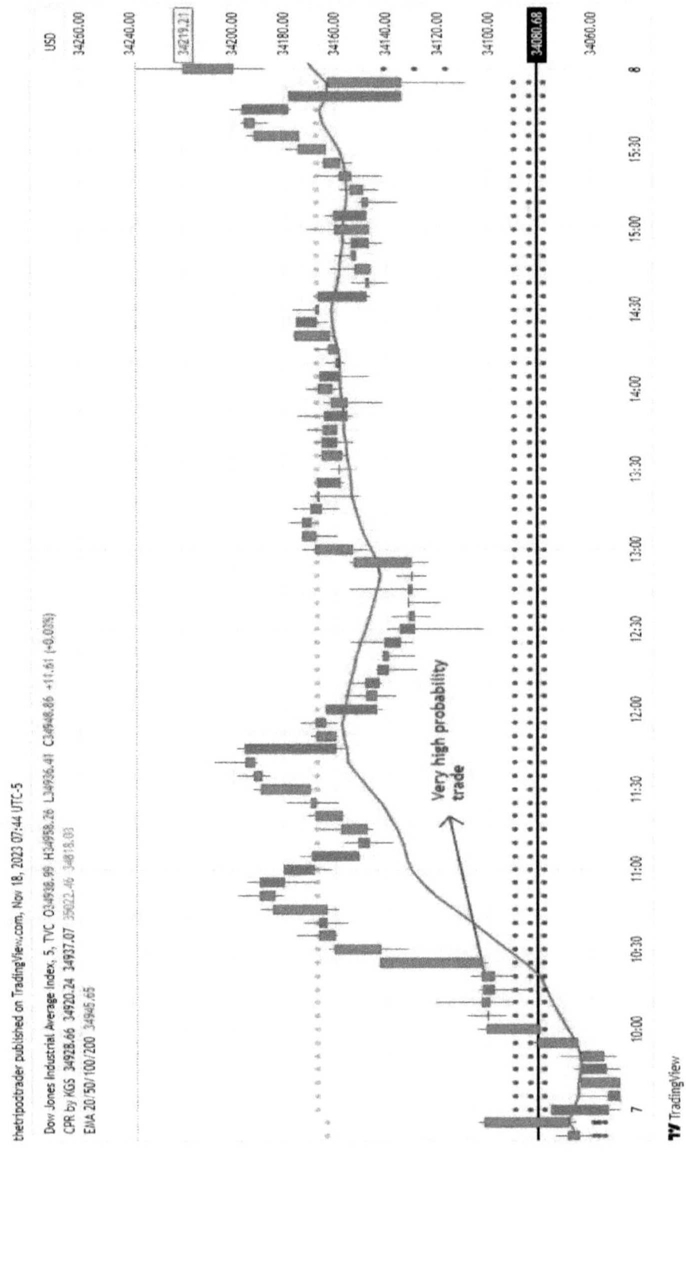
thetripodtrader published on TradingView.com, Nov 18, 2023 07:44 UTC-5
Dow Jones Industrial Average Index, 5, TVC
EMA 20/50/100/200
Very high probability trade
TradingView

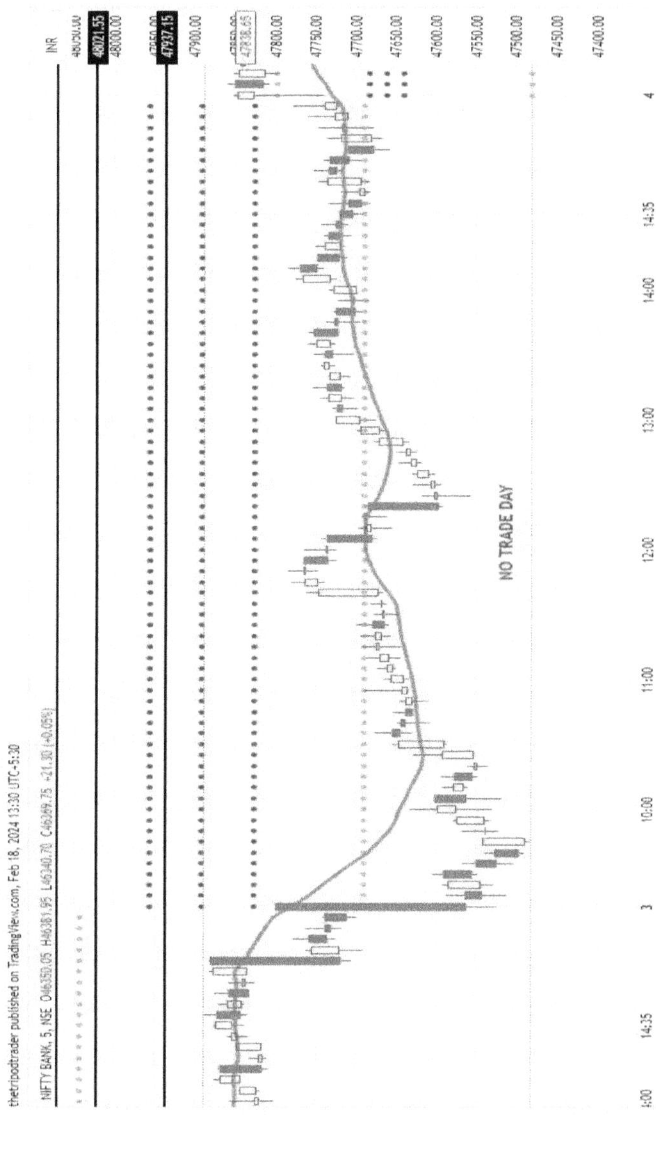
thetripodtrader published on TradingView.com, Feb 18, 2024 13:30 UTC-5:30
NO TRADE DAY
TradingView

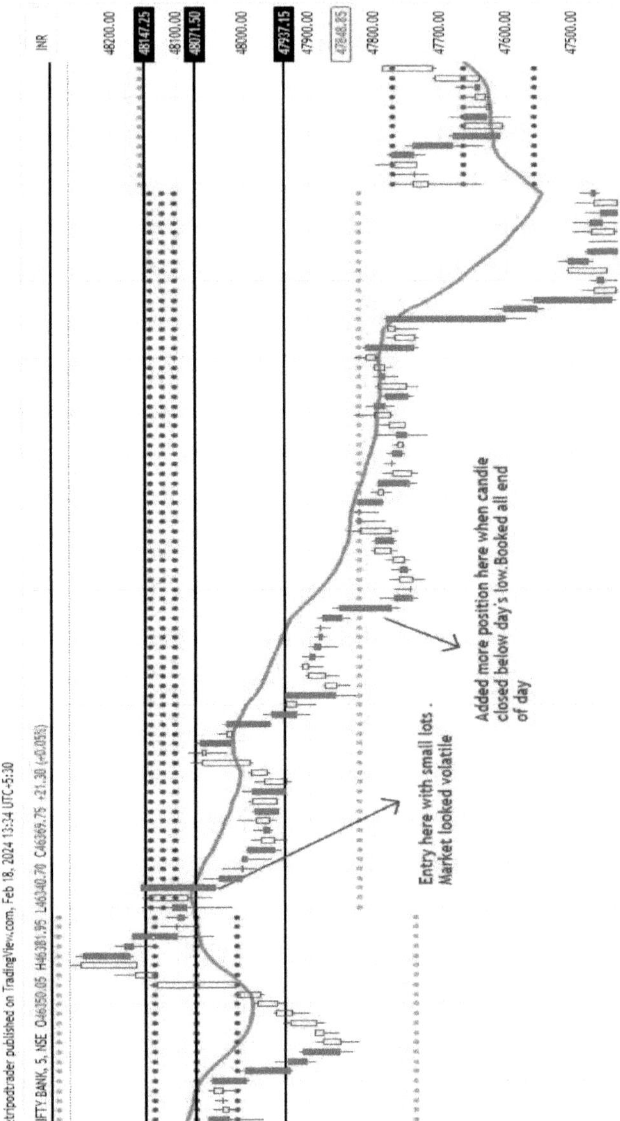
thetripodtrader published on TradingView.com, Feb 18, 2024 13:34 UTC+5:30
INR
48200.00
48147.25
48100.00
48071.50
48000.00
47937.15
47900.00
47848.85
47800.00
47700.00
47600.00
47500.00
Entry here with small lots . Market looked volatile
Added more position here when candle closed below day's low.Booked all end of day
14:00
14:40
8
10:00
11:00
12:00
13:00
14:00
14:40
9
10:00
TradingView

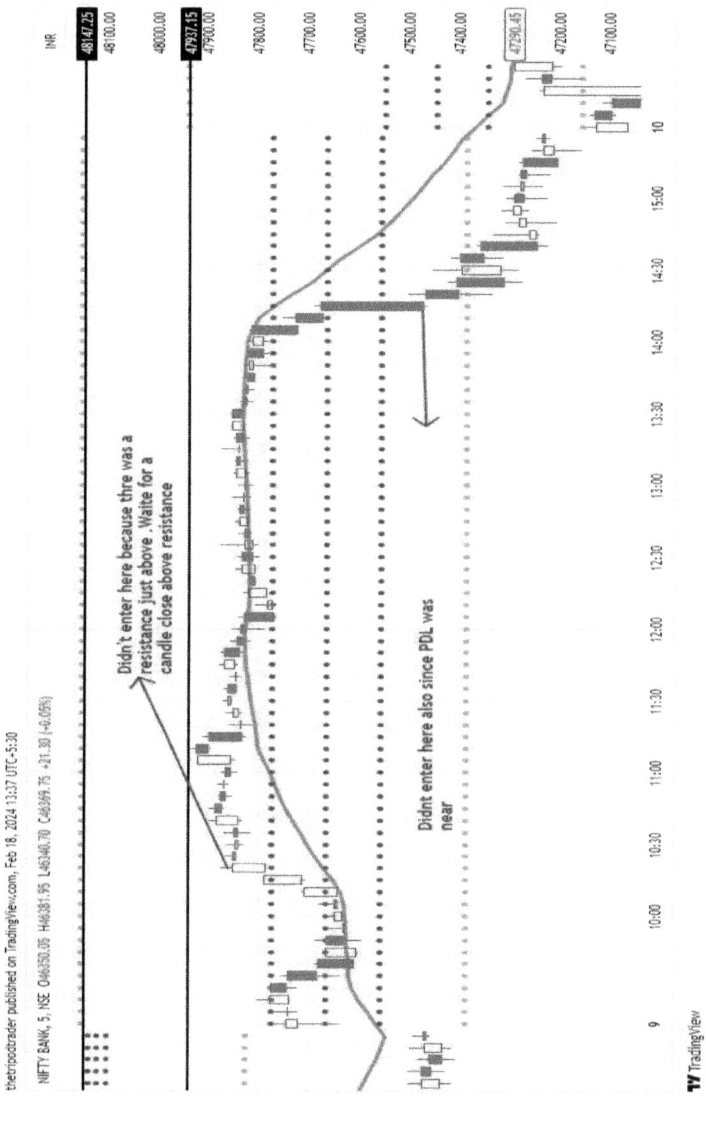
thetripodtrader published on TradingView.com, Feb 18, 2024 13:37 UTC-5:30
Didn't enter here because thre was a resistance just above . Waite for a candle close above resistance
Didnt enter here also since PDL was near
TradingView

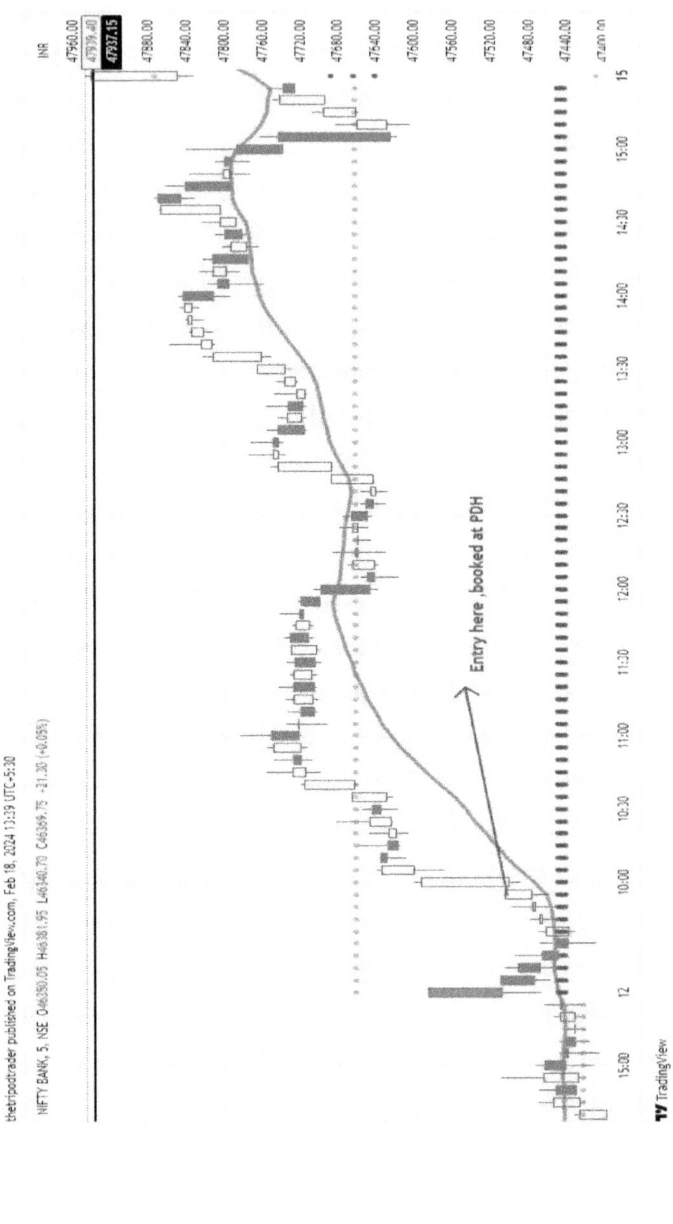
thetripodtrader published on TradingView.com, Feb 18, 2024 13:39 UTC-5:30
NIFTY BANK, 5, NSE O46350.05 H46381.95 L46340.70 C46369.75 -21.30 (+0.05%)
Entry here , booked at PDH
TradingView

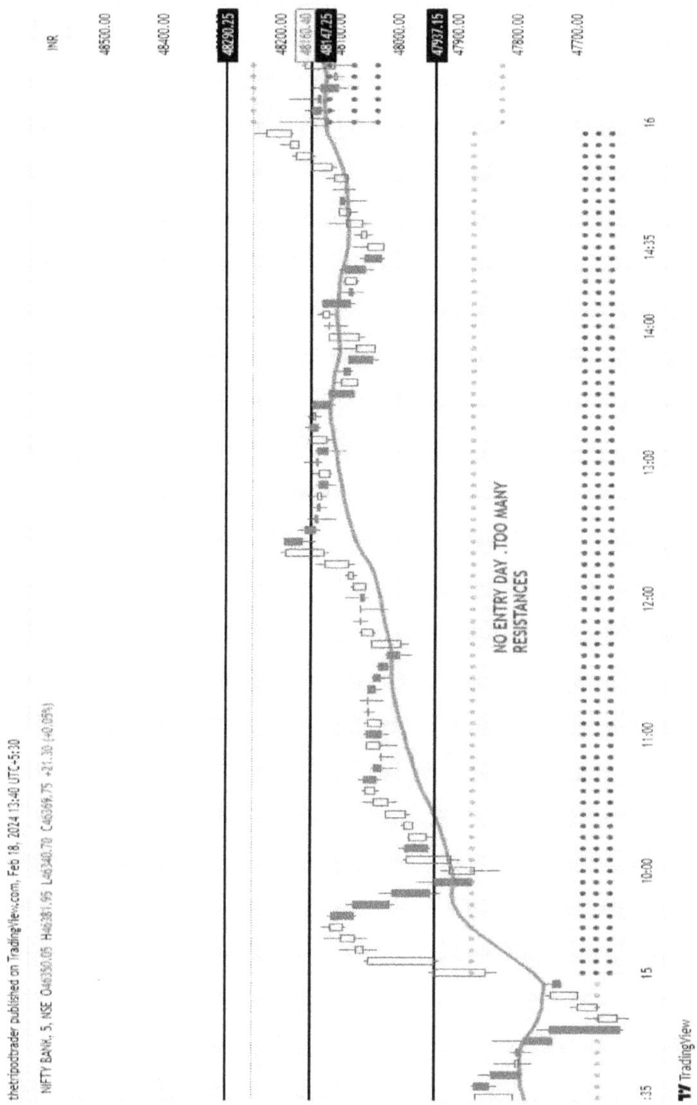
thetripodtrader published on TradingView.com, Feb 18, 2024 13:40 UTC-5:30
NO ENTRY DAY . TOO MANY RESISTANCES
48290.25
48147.25
47937.15
TradingView

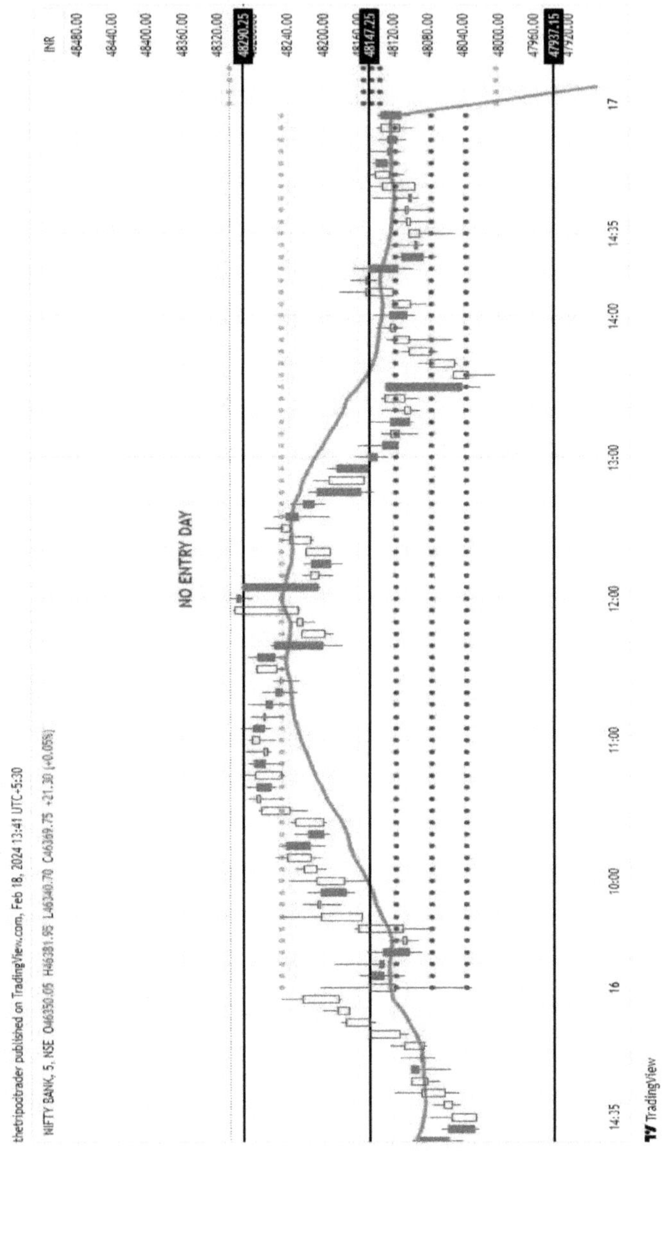
thetripodtrader published on TradingView.com, Feb 18, 2024 13:41 UTC+5:30
NO ENTRY DAY
48290.25
48147.25
47937.15
TradingView

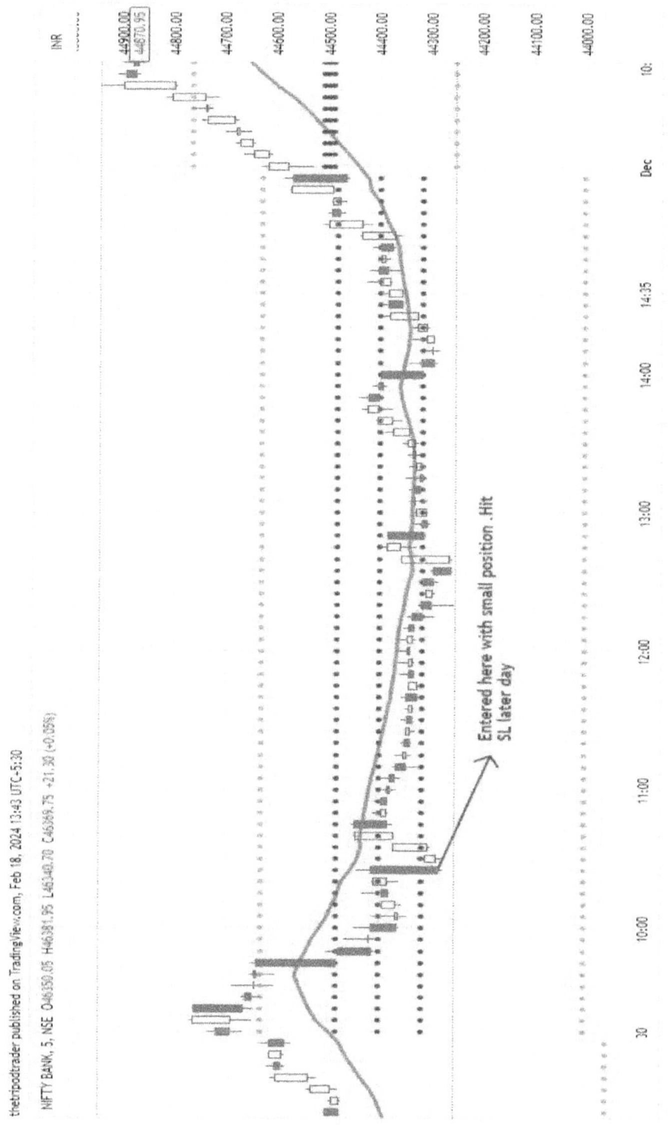
thetripodtrader published on TradingView.com, Feb 18, 2024 13:43 UTC-5:30
NIFTY BANK, 5, NSE O46350.05 H46381.95 L46340.70 C46369.75 +21.30 (+0.05%)
Entered here with small position .Hit SL later day
TradingView

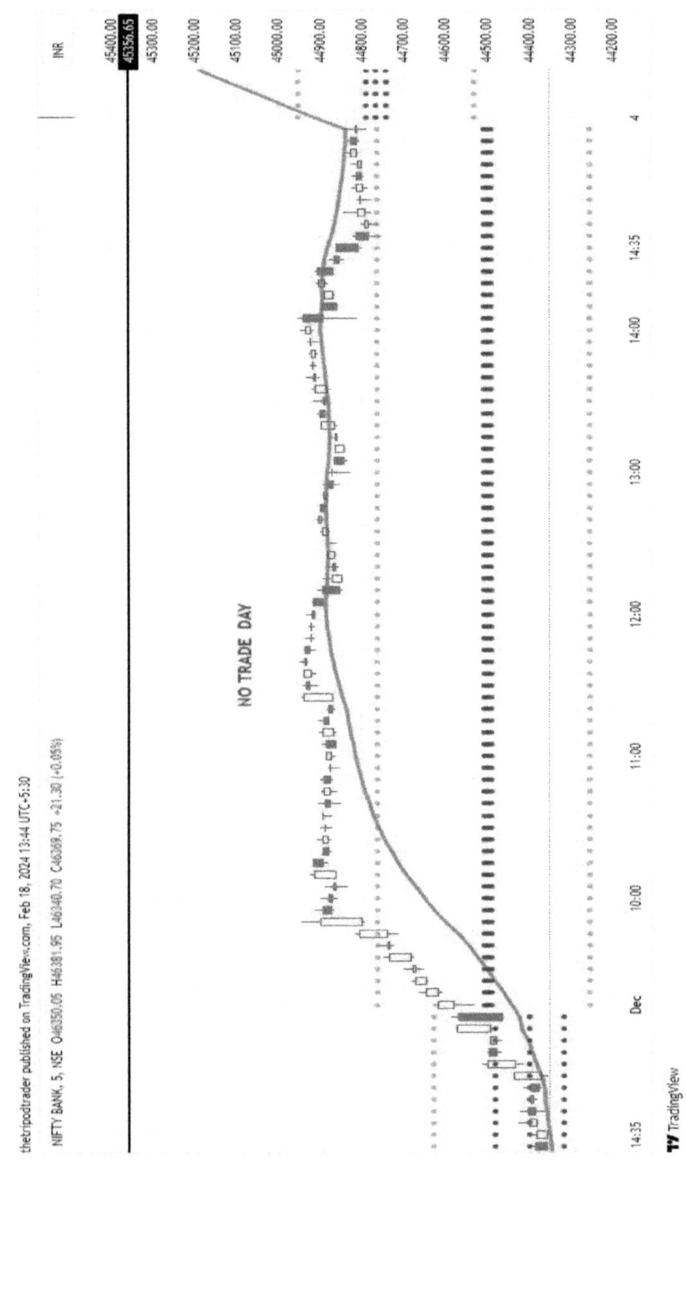
thetripodtrader published on TradingView.com, Feb 18, 2024 13:44 UTC-5:30
NIFTY BANK, 5, NSE O46350.05 H46381.95 L46340.70 C46369.75 +21.30 (+0.05%)
NO TRADE DAY
INR
45400.00
45356.65
45300.00
45200.00
45100.00
45000.00
44900.00
44800.00
44700.00
44600.00
44500.00
44400.00
44300.00
44200.00
14:35
Dec
10:00
11:00
12:00
13:00
14:00
14:35
4
TradingView

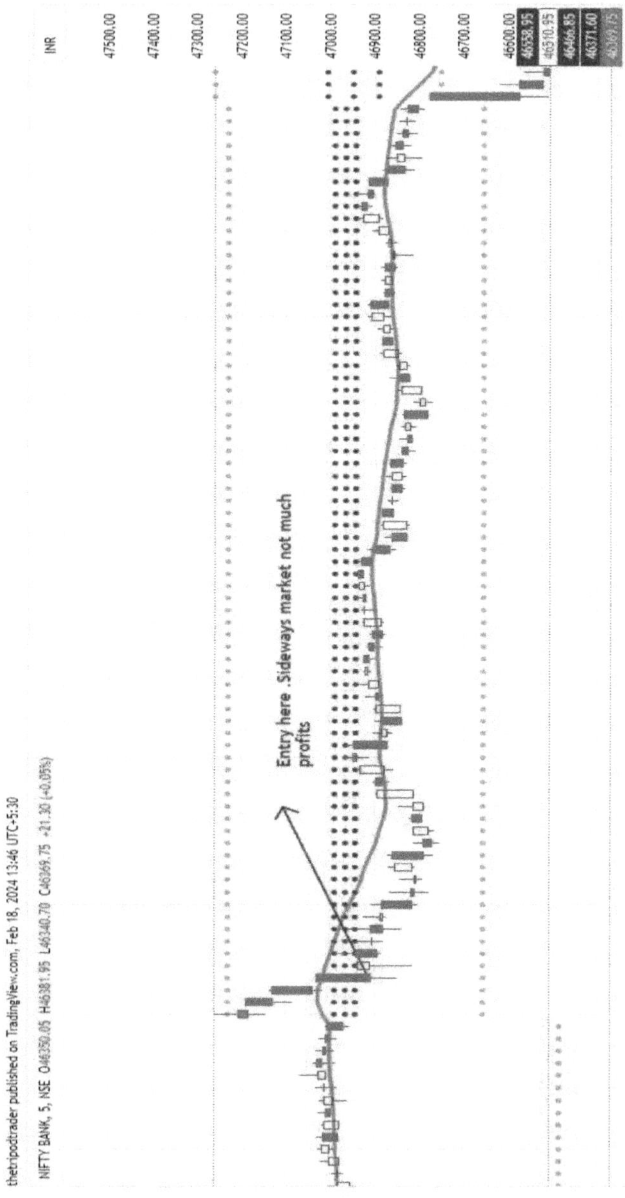

thetripodtrader published on TradingView.com, Feb 18, 2024 13:46 UTC-5:30
NIFTY BANK, 5, NSE O46350.05 H46381.95 L46340.70 C46369.75 +21.30 (+0.05%)
Entry here .Sideways market not much profits
INR
47500.00
47400.00
47300.00
47200.00
47100.00
47000.00
46900.00
46800.00
46700.00
46600.00
14:35
6
10:00
11:00
12:00
13:00
14:00
14:35
7
TradingView